When I first read, From Jilt to Joy, I thought my problems had been taken care of really, but I found that I didn't really forgive my abusers like I thought. When I read that I was suppose to forgive my abuser to be set free, I did it and finally I forgave my father for sexually abusing me when I was young. After I decided to forgive him I felt a weight being lifted off my shoulders.

I felt so good that I was able to forgive all the people that did bad things to me as a teenager. As I look back on those things they don't hurt as bad as they use to. All I can say is, "Thank you" to Mrs. Banks for writing such a badly needed book.

This book has a lot to offer and I would tell anyone that is hurting from the past to get out there and buy the book today, read it, and be set free as God intended us to be.

Kind regards, C.C.

I met you at the House of Praise and Workship in Greensboro this past Saturday, November 16. I purchased your book, From Juilt to Joy, and just wanted to let you know that I started reading it that night and could not put it down. I felt like you were talking straight to me on some issues. I really enjoyed meeting you and thank you for blessing of reading your book.

Sincerely, R. Stapleton

Having read From Jilt to Joy has made my soul rejoice. Izona has done a great and successful job in helping me to receive hope, confidence and a more positive outlook on my life once again. The book came to me just in time.

Sincerely, D.L.D.

Watch out! Expect to stay up a while. From Jilt to Joy is a must read! I couldn't put the book down. After reading it I have a closer walk to forgiveness. I also learned that childhood hurts could be healed.

Truly, Tammy

When I saw the title of the book, From Jilt to Joy, God spoke to my heart. I felt drawn to read the front and back cover. Then I got such peace and closer relationship with this book, I am also going From Jilt to Joy.

Blessing, Jennifer

When I read the book, From Jilt to Joy, I found hope for my situation through Christ Jesus. When Izona shared how she overcame her difficult experiences and trials, it gave me hope and encouragement to overcome my trials and tribulations. Those scriptures and prayers after each chapter have made a difference in my life.

Sincerely, Louise

I read the book from cover to cover in a very brief period of time, and found it to be a very well written book, expressed in a caring and loving manner. The inspiring and uplifting climax should be an encouragement to all women who are hurting or experiencing painful situations.

Martha Bruno, Minister, Writer, Religious Educator

from Jilt *to* Joy
Help for Hurting Women

from Jilt *to* Joy
Help for Hurting Women

A complete guide to overcoming rejection, hurts, anger, abuse, rape, deception, unforgiveness. Your invitation to enter into joy through the power of God

IZONA BANKS

Mall Publishing, Co.
THE PRINTED WORD THE PLANTED SEED

5731 Howard St., NIles, IL 60714

Copyright © 2002 Izona Banks
All rights reserved

Printed in the United States of America
Published by: Mall Publishing Company
5731 W. Howard Street, Niles IL 60714

Unless otherwise noted,
all scripture quotations are from
the King James Version (KJV) of the Holy Bible.

Cover Design: Andrew Ostrowski
Book Design: Theodore E. Mall

ISBN 0-9718964-1-0

For licensing/copyright information,
for additional copies or for use in specialized settings
Contact:
Izona Banks Ministry
P. O. Box 598, Demopolis, AL 36732
e-mail: Info@izonabanks.org
Web Site: www.izonabanks.org

Contents

Dedication..vi
Acknowledgment..vi
Foreword...vii
Introduction..ix
1. Peaks & Valley..1
2. Abuse..13
3. Curved Relationship..............................23
4. Deception..33
5. Prom...41
6. Traumatized..49
7. Better or Worse....................................57
8. Misconception.....................................67
9. Empty Vessel.......................................77
10. Complacent...87
11. Power of Forgiveness.............................95
12. Pursue Joy...105
Epilogue..117
End Notes...118

Dedication

I dedicate this book to my husband, two sons, two daughters, one daughter-in-law, one granddaughter, four grandsons, three great grand-sons, one great-grand-daughter, siblings, many relatives, and friends that have touched my life.

I also dedicate this book to my parents and oldest sister who have gone to be with Lord!

Acknowledgements

I acknowledge Father God, His son Jesus Christ, and the Holy Spirit, my helper. I wish to thank my many sisters and brothers in Christ for all of their prayers, support, and belief in me during the preparation of this project.

Thanks to my sons and daughters for their belief in me, and encouragement to pursue my life goal as a Christian Writer. Thanks to my special granddaughter and grandson, for helping me with the meals and chores, that I could spend more time writing.

Special thanks to my husband, for allowing me to write many late nights, also for his love and support. I thank God for Corey, all that he is, and all that he is going to achieve for the kingdom God.

Foreword

Not many people can bare their souls as readily as Izona Banks does in this book. She doesn't hide unpleasant reality and at the same time she constantly reminds readers that Jesus Christ is the healer of every deep pain and heartache. Izona Banks depicts her own sexual assault, but she does something even more important. She discusses her decision to forgive. Then she reminds us that forgiving those who hurt us is a choice. This is a powerful, poignant and uplifting book and worth reading.

Cecil Murphey
Author and co-author of 85 books
Including *Gifted Hands* (The Ben Carson Story),
Rebel With a Cause (Franklin Graham's autobiography).
His latest book is *The God Who Pursues*, published by
Bethany Press.

Introduction

By writing this book, From Jilt to Joy, which is drawn from my personal experiences, I hope that others might experience inner healing through the power of God. This book was born through much prayer for God to enable me to leave a legacy that will reach many souls in present and future generations. I later got a burning desire to help other hurting women after seeking God for inner healing for abused children and salvation for their abusers. During my research, interviews, and prayers, I discovered many women, similar to myself, have suffered abuse such as sexual harassment and rape, therefore experiencing rejection, depression, anger, fear, low self-esteem, and unforgiveness. I also discovered that various health problems are credited to unforgiveness.

Many hurting women want more than sweeping these experiences into their sub-conscious, going into denial, or holding the abuser in hostage by unforgiveness. There are a growing number of abused women in this country and around the world that want to know more about moving through hurting experiences into joyful victorious living.

Statistics cite undeniably the facts; strangers, family member, acquaintances, and neighbors abuse women and children every year.

This book includes biblical examples of sexual abuse, and references with permission from known authors on abuse and unforgiveness. After I confessed my own personal experiences of abusive situations and forgave my abusers, God set me free. I am inspired to share my story in this book with other hurting souls hopefully; they too can gain victory through the power of God.

Many names of people and places in the book have been changed in order to protect the identity.

Izona Banks, 2002

Chapter One

Peaks and Valleys

I was robbed of my innocence at age twelve. It took me almost fifty years to forgive my abuser. I went from being a joyful carefree young girl to one with many hurts and sorrows. I remember some high points from my childhood on the farm in Browns County, Alabama, near White Stone River, but unforgiveness, anger, fear, deep-seated rejection, and depression engulfed me like a cancer. By covering up the truth I became demon enslaved to self-righteousness, and pride. I believe God had a plan for my life even before birth, but Satan wanted me to take my life or ruin my testimony before God's purpose could be fulfilled.

According to Mom, Dad dreamed before conception that the next child would be a girl he should name Izona. I am the youngest of fifteen children, counting the miscarriages, but only six lived past the age of one month.

Dad seemed to have looked out for his family, because he built a house on Mom's land that she inherited from her grandparents before I made my arrival. He cut trees from the land to build the log cabin, with a large kitchen, two large bedrooms, and a smoke house to hang and cure the pork. The bedrooms had two beds in each one. Some of the children slept in the room with our parents, and the rest shared the other bedroom.

Dad and I must have enjoyed each other in our home during the short time we had together, because Mom often said, "Ellis loved his children. He would dress his babies, take them to church, and proudly show them to his family and friends." Mom must have loved Dad very much because when she discussed him her face became illuminated. Dad died at a young age leaving Mom with six children. Abraham was thirteen; Frances, eleven; Alice, six; Lawrence, five; Ned, three: I was six months old. Mom helped me to keep the memory of Dad fresh in my mind by talking about him often.

I created a fantasy world with Dad during my childhood. In my make-believe world I posed as Dad's little girl. In the real world I wished he could protect and offer me security. As a child I believed my Dad could have solved all of my problems, since in my imagination he was a perfect man. Mom and neighbors often shared the fact that Dad died for a few minutes, but came back, and preached his only sermon. They would quote him, "God called me to preach years ago; I didn't obey. Instead I ran by doing things of the world, but I can't leave this world until I obey His call." After preaching one sermon, they said he peacefully went to be with the Lord.

Mom kept the dress that I wore to Dad's funeral until my 10th birthday. She trusted me to keep up with the special little dress.

"Izona, take care of this dress; you wore it to your daddy's funeral."

"Okay, Mom. I will take good care of my baby dress."

I was excited because Mom finally thought I was mature enough to be trusted with this keepsake, but I got careless. I would hold the soft violet dress with white ribbon and lace trim in my hand as I spun around showing it to my friends in our neighborhood, "See my baby dress."

We ran, chased, tagged each other, and tossed the dress among us down near the river. It was during this time that we dropped the dress and kept playing. When we got tired of playing we left the area and went to a friend's house. I remembered the dress later that afternoon, but when I returned, it had disappeared. With the dress gone I felt a sense of loss because it connected me personally with my dad. Dad didn't even leave a picture for me to relate to. I depended on Mom's description of him.

Mom married Ben Baker when I was two years old. He moved us five miles away from our family's home to live with him. I vaguely remember when we began living with this tall slim man with slightly gray hair. We three younger children called him Daddy.

Mom and the older three children referred to him as Mr. Ben. He was the only daddy I can remember.

Daddy Ben had a large framed farmhouse that sat on a hill near White Stone River. His house had a real large kitchen, with a large room on each side. One of them was used for a smokehouse to cure the meat, the other was used for storage. We used the upstairs for storing can fruits, vegetables, and many other nonperishable foods.

Daddy Ben made a ladder for us to enter the attic. When we entered the living room through the front door, one large bedroom was on the left, and the other one on the right. We could enter our bedrooms from the outside without going through the front door. I can remember sleeping in the room with Mom and Daddy some nights when I was small. The children's room had a bed for the girls and one for the boys, but sometimes we used pallets on the floor when the weather was hot. During the 1940's we used paper from magazines to cover our walls, but in the early 1950's we changed to wallpaper. The house had a long porch that extended across the entire front. We had a good view of the river from our front porch.

Daddy and my brothers fished in the river; they kept some of the fish for the family, and sold the rest. They also hunted for game and deer that were used for food since we had access to a lot of land. We raised horses, mules, cattle, hogs, turkeys, ducks, chickens, and guineas. Daddy and my brothers used mules to pull the wagon. We plowed the fields to grow cotton, corn, oats, and many other kinds of vegetables.

Most of our food came from the farm. Daddy and my brothers killed the fowl, we gathered the eggs for our use, and marketed the rest. We milked the cows for milk, and butter; I kept the calves away while the older children did the milking.

Those fresh vegetables from our farm must have been healthy for us, since we didn't suffer a lot of illnesses. We picked berries in the spring and early summer. We canned berries for pies, made jelly, and jam. I can almost taste the cured ham and eggs served with homemade biscuits, baked in a wood-burning stove. We used stove-wood to heat the stove for cooking. I brought the wood into the kitchen, after my brothers chopped it into small pieces to fit in the wood stove.

We spread the homemade biscuits with butter and jelly or jam or sopped them in syrup. Daddy also raised the cane and made the syrup himself; he taught my brothers all of his skills. We drank buttermilk that was also prepared at home. We used horses for transportation, by pulling the wagon, and horseback riding. Daddy took the hogs, and cows to the stockyard for sale, except a few he kept for food. He took the cotton to the cotton gin in the fall, to separate the cotton from the seed for marketing. The whole family got new clothes and many kinds of treats when the profit came in from the crops.

Daddy's friends would ask, "Who is that you got with you, Ben?" He would reply with excitement, "This is Izona, my baby." I never heard him refer to me as his stepdaughter; that pleased me because by that time I understood the difference between a step-daddy and a biological daddy. Daddy introducing me as his baby gave me a feeling of acceptance. I can imagine that it also boosted his ego having a child that young, since he was twenty years Mom's senior.

The first spanking I can remember from Daddy was for playing a game with some kittens by putting them under a tub. I took a nap when I felt tired and forgot about them. It broke my heart when Daddy discovered the kittens had died during my nap. I believe he thought my intent was to harm them. He had cats; Mom brought our cats into the marriage. When they kept breeding, we had an overabundance of cats. The kittens must have died in their sleep because we didn't hear them make a sound.

I soon forgot about the spanking, but his words lingered with me for a long time. As he spanked me he said, "You are going to be a murderer before you become twenty-one."

Daddy spanked me the second time for hitting Ned, my brother on the head with a piece of stove-wood. Those are the only times I can remember him spanking me.

Alice and Mom did most of the cooking during my early years. Mom started teaching me how to cook at age seven after she became ill and required surgery. Her doctor put a limit on her lifting, meanwhile the other children and Daddy worked in the fields. I stayed home to help Mom with the housework and the meals. Since Daddy had health problems he could only have a small amount of sugar. The first thing I remember cooking was a cake with less sugar for Daddy. When Daddy came home to eat his dinner he noticed the lopsided cake on the table.

"I made you a cake, Daddy; do you want me to serve you a piece?"

"Sure, give me a slice after dinner."

It pleased me that a real person, an adult, wanted some of my cooking. Until that day my friends and I made mud cakes in our playhouse and had pretend parties. With shaky hands, I sliced a piece of cake for Daddy, and carefully placed it on his plate trying not to drop any crumbs on the table.

I wanted him to think, *She is quite a young lady, Nancy.* Nancy, my mom didn't make a sound, she just smiled broadly as I carried out her instructions on serving cake. Daddy put a piece of cake on his fork then slowly put it in his mouth. I watched closely, waiting for his approval. It seemed as if it took him all afternoon to respond. I cleared my throat, wrung my hands, and thought, *I hope he likes my cooking.*

"This is a delicious cake, Baby."

"Thank you Daddy, do you want me to make you another one?"

"No, you don't need to make another cake today."

"Okay, let me know when you want me to cook something else."

He could've been just trying to encourage me to continue to cook. Nevertheless, I kept watching Mom cook and copying until my cooking improved.

My family showed extra special treatment to me at Christmas; it was exciting. Alice, my older sister, and Mom did a lot of baking for the holidays. The homemade cakes and pies are still vivid in my mind today. The aroma from baking cakes filled the old farmhouse. I can still hear the crackling of the firewood and the smell of smoke coming from the kitchen as they started baking two weeks before Christmas. They bought crates of apples and oranges a few weeks before Christmas and stored them in the attic to use during the holidays. The fragrance of the fruit seeped throughout the house, and our entire family displayed enthusiasm as the holidays drew near.

Mom and Daddy often told us, "We will pay Santa Claus to bring you some presents if you are obedient." Even our extended family members tried to make the myth of Santa Claus seem as real as possible. To reinforce that Santa Claus had visited the children, Calvin, my uncle, would eat a slice of cake during the night on Christmas Eve, and put a few strands of his gray hair near his plate to trick the children.

He would say, "Oh! Look, Santa Claus must have had a slice of cake, because some of his hair is on the table."

All the children bubbled over with excitement, thinking Santa Claus came down the chimney to their house and brought the toys. Abraham, my oldest brother, often made me feel special when he would pay Santa Claus to bring me a big stick of peppermint candy and a doll for Christmas. I would run into his arms cheerfully and hug his neck. I often talk about the dolls and peppermint candy canes Abraham gave me during my childhood. The children went to bed early Christmas Eve; because they wanted to rise early Christmas morning to see what Santa Claus had left under the tree. Our family gave Santa Claus credit for the gifts we received at Christmas.

At age seven, Christmas began to be a sorrowful time for me. First, Daddy died a few days before the holidays. The next Christmas, Frances, my oldest sister got married and moved to Ohio which seemed so far from home. When Frances left to live with her husband, I dashed to my room and curled in a fetal position on my bed. My eyes were brimming with tears, as I spoke in a ragged voice, "Mom, my head hurts." I was trying to hide the sorrow I felt about Frances moving so far from home. Mom gave me a headache tablet, and I slept for several hours. Mom was so overwhelmed with her own emotions that I didn't want to reveal how deeply I was affected by Frances leaving home.

The very next Christmas, Lawrence, my brother, informed me that Abraham hid the gifts under the Christmas tree instead of Santa Claus. This happened just a few days before Christmas. I decided against telling Mom and my older siblings that I knew about the Santa Claus myth, but that didn't work. Lawrence told the entire family that I knew they played Santa Claus.

"Why are ya'll going to keep surprising her? She knows there is no Santa Claus."

Christmas didn't seem the same to me after the sadness, hurts, and the disappointments that surrounded those three Christmas holidays.

"Well, since you don't believe in Santa Claus anymore, this will be the last gift he will bring you," announced Abraham. He had no idea how dismayed I felt because of Lawrence, my brother's disloyalty. Even though I got presents for Christmas, I missed expecting to see Santa with his sleigh being pulled by reindeer to our farmhouse.

After Daddy's death and Frances moving away, Mom's responsibilities increased. Frances had helped with the washing, ironing, and cleaning, and she also disciplined us younger children. Mom became the disciplinarian, homemaker, priest of the home, and manager of the farm after Daddy's death. She also taught Sunday school, and participated in church activities such as picnics, and box suppers. The ladies used the box suppers to earn money for the church. They would prepare a meal and carry it to the church in a box; a gentleman would pay to eat out of the box of his choice.

As a disciplinarian, Mom took her job seriously. These are some of her favorite quotes: "Don't spare the rod and spoil the child." "Love your neighbor as yourself." "Do unto others as you would have them do unto you." When Mom actually applied the rod, I soon modified my behavior.

I have never laid claim to being an expert in the field of agriculture. It took me a long time to finish chopping one row of cotton because I would stand and daydream about living a better life in Milwaukee, Wisconsin. After reading the name Milwaukee I decided it must be a nice place to live. One morning, Mom was tired of fussing at me about chopping faster. She held a switch in one hand and her hoe in the other as she walked toward me.

"I am tired of fussing, and begging you to chop faster," she sighed.

I thought to myself, *Stop fussing if you are tired?* Mom didn't tolerate her children talking back out loud. In those days parents could give children a certain look and they would become obedient. As the thought entered my mind, Mom stopped begging.

"I will take your row half way, go back to the end and start mine; if I catch you before you finish, I am going to put this switch on your rump."

I let her catch up with me before I finished chopping my row. As she applied the switch, she stated, "No police will have to whip my children; I will do it myself to keep you out of jail and hell. Besides, if a person won't work, he will steal."

As priest of the home, she carried us to Sunday school and church, taught us to memorize scriptures, and sing praises to God. She taught us the Ten Commandments, and always told us if someone mistreats us pray for them, and don't try to get revenge. God will take care of them if you hold your peace and obey the word of God. She put a foundation of the Word of God in us while we were young, taught us to fear, and obey Him. As we grew up it became a part of our lives.

Mom organized chores for us children in the house and yard; when we finished, we went to the fields. We brought cool, crystal clear water home from a spring in pails. I was glad when some of the men from our neighborhood installed a pump in our yard. We would pump the water, bring it home in buckets, fill a big black pot, heat it, and wash the clothes in a washtub by hand on a wash board. After washing we hung the clothes outside on a clothesline to dry, we also used the same pot to heat our bath water. Since we didn't own a lawn tractor, we cut the grass with a hoe and swept it out of the yard.

Mom made sure we beautified our surroundings with flowers. We painted the fence white with lime rock mixed with water. She always reminded us of how blessed we were. She taught us how to sew our own clothes. During rainy or cold weather we stayed inside, and made dresses, curtains, and bedspreads instead of going to the fields. We also did crochet, embroidery, and many crafts for the home, which kept us busy.

Mom taught us to be proud, but I became too filled with my own worth that it became a downfall in my life. "Have some pride. How would that look to people? What will people think? Make sure you change your under clothes, because you might have an accident and go to the hospital. If the underwear is dirty how will that look to people?"

I tried to conceal my shortcomings, because of pride. Pride will cause great consequences. Although I memorized scriptures, I still needed to humble myself. According to James, "God resisteth the proud, but giveth grace unto the humble, (James 4:6 b)." Solomon stated in Proverbs 11:2, "Pride goeth before destruction, and a haughty spirit before a fall." Mom taught us many things about God and His word, although it was much later in life when I realized pride is sinful. Pride is one of the sins that God hates. It is ok to have a happy feeling about an accomplishment, but sin comes in when we think we are superior to others and take all of the credit from God. Nebechadnezzar walked in the royal palace of the kingdom of Babylon. At the end of twelve months he boasted about what he had done by his own power. As a result, God allowed him to dwell with the animals until he realized God rules over all men. We don't have anything to be proud of because God can give and take away whenever He desires. When I saw in God's word the examples of unfavorable experiences because of pride, it caused me to seek God by humbling myself. It is wise for us to humble ourselves before God. When He humbles us, He might take us lower than we desire to go. According to Solomon in Proverbs 29:23, "A man's pride shall bring him low: but honor shall uphold the humble in spirit."

Think about your life; are you filled with pride? You don't have to fall into the hands of an angry God. God loves us. His expectation for us is to live according to His word. Therefore, ask Him to search your heart and reveal if there's pride in your life. If he shows that you have the sin of pride, pray for deliverance and humble yourself before God. If we humble ourselves He will elevate us in due time.

Chapter two

Abuse

During my early years, I heard a common saying, "Boys will be boys.". I often thought, *What does that statement mean? And why not, 'Girls will be girls?'* Boys would sometime touch a girl's breast and react in amusement but to her it was discomfort. Regardless of the girl's ages she sensed, s*omething is wrong with this.* Today this type treatment is termed "sexual harassment."

I can remember as my friends and I played near the river, some white men drove down the river in their big boats, and yelled out at us, "I want some of your -----."

I could not understand why grown-ups would do something to cause that kind of fear in young girls. After that experience we ran home whenever we heard a motorboat. Laws seemed to have had a double standard at that time in history. The lawmakers didn't seem to care about protection for a black girl; therefore we lived in fear. Many years before the laws changed, it seem as if the laws didn't have much to do with the woman or her feelings.

Many cases of sexual harassment, even rape, went unreported because the law would not protect women's rights. I can remember inappropriate advances made to me while in the work place, instead of reporting it to the Better Business Bureau or the authorities, I told Larry, my husband. He went with me to pick up my last check, to quit the job, and hope to find another one. At that time in history we felt defenseless. As a result, I learned a trade, opened my own business, and I never saw my tormentor again.

Date rape is difficult to prove, because in many cases girls are made to feel that it's their fault. If someone touches, caresses or keeps trying to have sex without permission, this is a sexual crime. The girls knew their stories of the rape would be questioned so they suppressed the incident instead of making a report. Some parents didn't want their daughter going through the extra trauma of being on the witness stand to face their abuser and the cross examination of the defense attorney.

I came close to an experience of incest with James, a male relative that had visited our home. It happened similar to the story about Amnon and Tamar, his half sister that is recorded in II Samuel, chapter 13. Amnon, David's son tricked Tamar, his half sister into cooking for him. He took advantage of her kindness by pretending he was sick. She cooked his food, carried it to him as a devoted sister would do for her brother, since she believed his story. As a result, Amnon used that opportunity to rape her.

Sometimes Mom allowed James to come stay a few weeks with us. He would sleep in the bed with my brothers; I slept in another bed. I awoke when I felt a sizable hand fondling my thigh. My heart began to race, my eyes widened in alarm, and I breathed heavily as I tried to scream. He put his shaking hand over my mouth and said in a low trembling voice, "Be quiet" Then he quickly moved back to my brother's bed. I broke out in a cold sweat as chills ran down my spine. My stomach knotted, and salty tears rolled into my mouth, and onto my pillow.

I reasoned, *If I hadn't woke up when I did he would have hurt me, or who knows what else.* Through the eyes of an eight-year-old, James seemed gigantic at age sixteen. The grace of God spared me, not just because I said this prayer each night before I went to bed. "God lay me down to sleep. If I should die before I wake, I pray the Lord my soul will take." It is because His grace is so amazing. My hurts continued and I accumulated unforgiveness as well as anger, fear, and low self-esteem. I am sharing these fearful experiences only for the sake of ministry; I am delivered by the power of God.

Not long after, I had another experience. One day while walking and skipping along the dusty road to our house from the country store, I had an encounter with Mr. Eugene Simon, our neighbor. The store was about a mile and a half from our home. As I passed by the field where Mr. Eugene plowed his crop, I waved a friendly hello to him the way Alabamians do.

He charged over near the road where I walked. "Come go down by the spring with me. I want you to do something for me."

I felt comfortable with him. After all he lived in our neighborhood as long as I can remember. I thought *He wanted me to take some milk or some other beverage to his wife from the spring.* The spring served as a refrigerator. We would place whatever beverage we wanted to keep cool in the spring, and took it out as needed.

"Yes sir, I will gladly do you a favor." We began walking toward the spring through the woods near the river.

I skipped along behind him making small talk. "Are those plums?"

He took an old red and white plaid, sweaty rag from his dusty, faded blue overall's packet; wiped the perspiration that streamed down his face. When he turned and faced me he had a peculiar stare in his eyes and spoke with a trembling voice. A foul smell of tobacco, garlic, fish, and burned cabbage all combined gave me a sick feeling in my stomach as he finally answered. "No those are sloes. They will be ripe in August. Are you going to lie down?"

His eyes seemed more peculiar; with shaky hands he moved closer toward me. After realizing his ungodly motive, my knees felt weak and shaky; my hair seemed to stand up on my head; a prickling sensation struck a nerve in my spine. I finally decided running had to be my best alternative, so I ran as fast as my bare feet could take me down that hot sandy road to our house. My heart seemed to have performed flip-flops, and certainly I was exhausted.

I finally entered my safe haven. That seemed like the longest mile that I have ever run. I told my adult sisters and sister-in-law of the frightful experience that I had encountered with Mr. Eugene. They must not have known the extent of the fear, hurt, shame, anger, guilt, and emotional trauma I had experienced. If they had known, I believe their response would have been different. In my terror I needed them to empathize with me. Their response caught me of guard. "Don't tell Mama, because she will have him put under the jail." Their expression, "under the jail" meant to have him put in jail for a long time. My heart grew heavy and I felt overwhelmed with disappointment that no one shared my hurt and humiliation. *Who else can I turn to for comfort,* I thought. I ran behind our house as tears gushed from my eyes, trying to keep them from seeing me cry. Shame, guilt, fear, and anger never left me, and I was stunned by their reaction, which left me bewildered.

What if he does go to jail for a long time? He wanted to harm me, I thought. I developed an unfavorable opinion of men because of the way some treated me. I harbored unforgiveness. With so many disappointments in life, it left me quite hostile. I didn't love myself, and thought others felt the same way about me. I would fight if children said something I didn't like, which happened quite often. I felt unloved, rejected, and unimportant, because I saw the ones I loved didn't have time for my problems. I built walls in my life early for protection, but underneath the walls I really wanted unconditional love and acceptance.

In the last few years I have interviewed women from many different walks of life. In my finding, many cases of sexual harassment and rape never got reported because in some cases relatives and acquaintances did the abusing. Sexual abuse can have a lasting, adverse effect on a person if they fail to deal with it properly. When we open up, tell what we have gone through to someone we trust to have unconditional love, and forgive the abuser, it will allow healing to begin. In addition to interviewing women from different ages, social, and ethnic backgrounds, as well as having counseled in a crisis pregnancy center for eight years, I discovered many of their experiences are similar to mine. Some things hurt so much until one might put them so deep into the subconscious and refuse to remember. A few things all of the women had in common were low self-esteem, anger, unforgiveness, and some suffer from denial and repression at some time since the abuse.

According to Papalia and Olds, authors of *A Child's World*, "The developing ego, or self-concept of school-age child is threatened on all sides. To combat anxiety, children may develop defense mechanisms, many of which persist throughout adult life. These mechanisms include: Repression - In anxiety-producing situations, children may repress, or block, feelings that they formerly may have expressed freely. These emotions are now so raw and uncomfortable that they cannot let them rise to consciousness."[1]

This quote sounds much like how I handled my abuse, as well as some of the women that shared their experiences. I put up a defense device in the form of denial for many years. I had very low tolerance of rape offenders; therefore I reacted by pacing the floor, eyes narrowed with contempt, and spoke with bitter resentment when I watched a movie that presented a rape scene. During a jury duty hearing of a rape trial a few years ago, the attorney asked everyone to please stand if they knew anyone personally that had been raped. After being stupefied for a few minutes, I finally stood up, admitting I knew someone that had been victimized by a rapist. I began to do research on many kinds of abuse, trying to understand my reaction to this hideous crime.

I wrote newsletters about many different kinds of abuse and mailed them to two hundred readers each month for two years, requesting prayer for the abused children and those who violated them. I began to desire salvation for the abuser, and deliverance for abused children. I didn't quite understand the urgency within me for inner healing of abused children. I prayed, "God please reveal to me what is in my heart that I need to get right with you." The more I prayed the greater the urgency became for deliverance of sexually abused children and salvation for their abusers.

Every time I attempted to write about sexually abused children, a lump rose up in my throat, and I would stop typing. I would stay away from the computer for a few weeks, trying not to think about sexually abused children.

The urgency I felt to receive deliverance and inner healing wouldn't go away. Finally one day I attempted once more to write about sexually abused children. I began to shake, and the lump in my throat got bigger. Salty tears rolled into my mouth while I sobbed, shook hysterically, and ran into Larry's arms.

"What is wrong with you? Please tell me what is wrong with you," he pleaded.

I kept shaking uncontrollably. The lump kept getting larger in my throat. Finally the gigantic lump burst out through my mouth like water rushing over a dammed up river. Larry held me close to him as I told him the whole story that I had denied for so many years.

I was twelve years old asleep in my bed in our country home when Billy, an older teenage acquaintance, who would visit my brothers sometime, raped me. It happened one night after his visit. He usually would stay about one hour, but that night he claimed he had to leave early and we went to bed. I always felt uncomfortable in the presence of Billy, because he had a devious smile, and would laugh about his wrong actions. He thought it was funny how his daddy would brag about getting him out of jail regardless of how often he got arrested. He spent more years in jail than as a free man. He didn't care to earn his money from earnest employment, and would laugh about how he would try to lie his way out of trouble. It seemed as if he didn't have a conscious. He finally learned the lesson much later in life, which I will discuss in later chapters.

Meanwhile, our house that I grew up in had an outside entrance to the bedrooms, in addition to the one from the living room. During Billy's visit the night he raped me, he must have noticed the door had a latch that could be opened from the outside by inserting a small slender stick through the crack. He snuck back, unlatched the door, got into my bed, and started to sexually abuse me. I felt something touching me in an uncomfortable way. I was too frightened to scream or move for a few seconds. I finally realized that a man was in my bed robbing me of my innocence. I felt helpless, but with cold, trembling, hands I got enough strength to hit, scratch, and bite him. I watched him jump on his horse and ride off in the bright moonlight.

That experience terrified me; I kept all that hurt inside for many years. I would get a sick feeling to think of him; so I just suppressed the experience, hoping I would never have to see him again. I will share later how Billy touched my life as an adult. Mom asked the next day, "What's wrong with you, why are you so quiet?" Ashamed, I answered, "I don't want to talk about it."

I was ill at ease in the presence of older boys, because my trust had been destroyed. I thought when I didn't remember the experience any longer it would be all right. The pain left my body, but the emotional pain, inner turmoil, distrust, unforgiveness, low self-esteem, and anger became a real problem. There seemed to be no relief. After I didn't receive love and understanding when Mr. Eugene attempted to abuse me, I thought, there *is no need to go to anyone for help, especially if the perpetrator is an acquaintance.* I read my Bible, but could not forgive. I didn't want to forgive because my life had many hurts, and disappointments. My inner healing would not come. Many times we justify our unforgiveness, but until we forgive there will be neither inner healing nor peace and joy in our lives. Satan can cause us to destroy our own happiness when we harbor shame and guilt and refuse to forgive those he has caused to hurt us. I felt rejection. I really missed my Dad and longed for the protection he could have provided had he been alive. I thought my mother, older sisters, and brothers would have offered a little more protection. I continued to have problems forgiving because I didn't know how to forgive.

I have learned that Satan can only do to us what God allows. But if God allows negative things to happen to people that love him, and are called for his purpose, He will let bad things work for the good. Those situations that God allows Satan to bring upon us can be used for God's glory. If we give God permission to work freely in our lives, He can use negative situations in our lives to help other hurting women. God is very intelligent, he allows us to make choices, but many times the ones we make are not to our advantage.

Some women that I interviewed stated that a stepfather, stepbrother, other family members, or an acquaintance forced their attention on them. They kept quiet about it for many years and blamed themselves. Any time a sexual act takes place without both parties' consent, it's rape and not the victim's fault. False guilt, shame, low self-esteem, and unforgiveness will destroy one's happiness. When we keep our feelings within, it allows us to think our hurts are worst than everybody else's. By sharing our problems with other hurting women we can empathize with each other.

It is a fact that it hurts when someone takes away a person's innocence, but how we handle the negative situations makes the difference. If we give God permission to work freely in our lives, He will heal us completely. Too many negative experiences and unforgiveness can cause physical and emotional problems. Shame, pride, and sometimes fear cause us to keep our hurts inside and allow a bitter, unforgiving spirit to take up residence in our hearts. With so many emotions bundled up inside, one might take their frustrations out on loved ones but this is not the answer. God is able and willing to heal the anger, depression, low self-esteem, unforgiveness, and all that follows rape and incest.

If you can identify with any of the experiences mentioned, and want to be set free, God is willing to make you a new creature. Even if a child was conceived, pray that the Holy Spirit will help you and your family to love the child as if the pregnancy were planned. Pray this prayer if it expresses the desires of your heart.

Dear Heavenly Father,
Help me to decide to forgive my abuser who has taken away my innocence, and left me with all of the responsibility. Please forgive me of all my sins, wash me in your blood. Jesus, come into my heart and be Lord of my life. Holy Spirit, please enable me to live for my Heavenly Father until the day I die. Thank you in Jesus' name, Amen.

When we forgive our abusers we will experience tremendous freedom in our own lives. But it takes the power of God and time, to complete the inner healing.

Chapter Three

Curved Relationships

"Everything that shines is not gold." "You can't judge a book by its cover." "The grass always seems greener on the other side of the fence." "A stitch in time saves nine." "You can tell a tree by its fruit." These were favorite sayings of Mom. I might have spared myself many hurts and disappointments if I had understood these wise sayings. She always tried to prevent me from going through certain hardships in life, even though each one of us has to bear our own crosses in this life. If we walk through what life offers and learn the lesson that's in it for us, as a result we will certainly come out a much stronger person.

Now I understand that many things and people are not what they seem at first sight. You have to get to know a person by building a relationship, just as you have to read a book to know what is inside. If we learn the lesson in life when we have our first test, it will prevent us from repeating the same test or making the mistakes. I met the love of my life at an early age, but kept looking for the end of the rainbow or the grass that always seemed greener on the other side of the fence. Sometimes, by looking for something that I read about in a fairy tale, I over looked the genuine. When all else failed I realized Larry Clark and I loved each other from early childhood. We traveled in circles but always got back together as our story unfolded.

This is how I started the boomerang relationship of my life. My second grade class had a school play, and after school Larry, and I became childhood sweethearts. The character I played called for me to wear a big floppy brown hat. After school I decided to wear my hat home instead of carrying it in my bag with the rest of my attire that I used for the play. As I walked in the narrow path through in the woods, the crackling sounds behind me sounded creepy. The brown, red, and yellow dried leaves covered the path. The noise seemed to get louder and louder as something or someone, got closer to me. It sounded like footsteps. My heart pounded as I got up enough nerve to look around to check out the noise. When I finally turned around, to my surprise I saw Larry Clark, a little boy from my school. After he got a little closer to me, he started to make small talk.

"That is a funny hat you are wearing."

"Thank you, Larry." His little black high top string up shoes crushed the leaves as he walked closer to me. He wore starched overalls and a plaid shirt with his pockets filled with pecans. We both seemed very self-conscious as I looked into his pretty brown eyes. He ran a little closer nervously gave me a big kiss on my cheek. Just as his lips left my cheek we looked and saw Mr. Jones, a friend of our families. We looked in each other eyes. I thought, *we are in big trouble.*

Larry ran fast toward his house with pecans falling out of his pocket. That kiss seemed so special, and I smiled whenever I thought of his warm little lips on my cheek. The only thing that spoiled the mood of that special kiss was the fact that Mr. Jones might tell our secret. Whenever he came to our house after Larry kissed me, I was afraid to go out to play because I thought if he got alone with Mom he would tell. I held a special place in my heart for Larry. He was my favorite childhood sweetheart. He supplied me with plenty of pecans. He seemed to enjoy running up to me, reaching in his pocket and giving me some of his pecans. I was disappointed when he moved and went to a different school. After he changed school, I only saw him on Sunday after services and other church gatherings. We talked every chance we got.

At thirteen I met Andy Richardson, another cute boy, at a church social. He rode up near me on his shiny black horse with white spots. He twiddled the long gold jive chain that was attached to a pocket watch. His black and white striped jitterbug pants, and black shirt matched his horse. In the late 1940's and early 1950's horses were a popular ride for young preteens and teenagers in our circle. I had problems keeping my eyes off him. He and his horse stood out in the crowd with all that black and white.

He gracefully dismounted and extended his hand toward mine with self-assurance, "My name is Andy Richardson, what's yours."

"I am Izona. I am glad to meet you."

"May I sit with you?"

"Yes, you may."

"Where have you been hiding? I haven't seen you around very much."

"I usually go to church, school functions, and occasionally to a movie."

Andy began talking to me regularly, and Larry seemed uneasy. Andy told me he wanted to visit me some Sunday afternoons. One day after Sunday school, Andy and I walked to the Jones' pump for a drink of water. I agreed to be his friend. Then, Larry appeared from nowhere.

"I thought you were my girl. Make up your mind who you want, me or Andy."

After thinking for a few minutes, I responded real low, "Andy."

Larry bolted off, unhappy; Andy and I talked as we returned to the church.

I thought of the sadness in Larry's eyes that night at home. I remembered the kiss on my cheek after the school play. I decided I still held a special place in my heart for Larry. The next week when I saw Larry he told me he still wanted me to be his girl. I assured him that I liked being his friend. I had a problem with my two boyfriends or they had one; I enjoyed the attention. The next week Andy saw Larry and me talking, and came near us stony-faced, "You have to decide if you want Larry or me."

It seemed proper to have Andy as a friend, but my relationship with Larry had special meaning. After taking a breath, I finally said, "I'm sorry Andy, Larry and I have been friends since second grade. I treasured his friendship." Andy let out a loud breath, and walked away.

Larry and I continued a close friendship during our early teen years. Andy moved north and probably went on with his flashy lifestyle. I felt happy when Larry and I went to the same elementary school. But in spite of us attending different high schools, we still managed to keep in touch. During our early teens, he found excuses to get a chance to see me. Sometimes he drove Mom home from town and helped unload our groceries. His broad smile caused me to blush when I looked in his brown eyes. It seemed as though we could understand each other with just a look. The tender feeling I felt for Larry helped me to rebuild my trust in boys after the negative experiences. He never forced his affection on me.

One Saturday afternoon while he helped Mom bring the groceries into the kitchen he said, "I want to come to visit you tomorrow."

"I won't be home. I am going to church with my family. Anyway, I'm not allowed to receive gentlemen-company until I am sixteen."

"Just stay home from church and I will visit you early in the day."

Sunday morning finally came and I thought h*ow could I manage to stay home from church? I wanted to see Larry.* "Mom, may I stay home today, I have a headache."

"Yes, since you are not going to church, cook dinner," Mom replied.

Excitement filled the house, as I made my bed and washed the breakfast dishes. Larry came riding up on Sparkle, his reddish-brown horse with a white spot in his forehead.

"Hello, here I am."

"Hi Larry, get down, come in and have a seat."

He tied his horse to a post, came over, and sat on the porch swing beside me.

We sat, swung and talked until Mom came home from church. I rushed in to the kitchen and started to make a fire in the wood-stove. The time seemed to have passed fast because I enjoyed his company. Mom dashed through the kitchen door, grabbed her head and made a long blow. I had entertained Larry instead of cooking dinner. My toes curled tightly in my shoes as I struggled to
control my voice.

"Mom, I'm sorry I didn't cook yet. I will have dinner ready in a few minutes." "Larry is determined to visit you. He is so persistent about asking for permission regardless to how many times I say no. Go and entertain him; you will be sixteen in a few months. That boy has a lot of nerve; he seems nice, but I am afraid he is going to be like his daddy."

Mom gave Larry permission to visit me on Sunday afternoon, Wednesday and Friday nights, but he had to leave before 9:00 P.M. or she would come where I was entertaining and say, "It's bed time." He would obey that rule, ask for his hat, and go home. Larry had a curfew also. I hated to see him leave so early because what we had seemed to be more than fascination. Our relationship continued and we grew closer until we allowed pride, stubbornness and unforgiveness to caused us to break-up. Larry came to visit me a few days before Christmas during my sophomore year of high school.

"Izona, I am going to ask Mrs. Nancy for permission to take you out Christmas night."

"Where are you going, Larry?"

"To the honky-tonk."

"I'm sorry, Larry. Mom won't allow me to go there."

His face got flushed with indignation, and spoke in grudging tones, "Okay! I will see you the day after Christmas."

Arrogantly impassive, voice dripping with spite, I slowly responded, "If you can't come to see me Christmas Day, don't come back at all." He refused to change his mind and went out with his friends instead of visiting with me on Christmas Day. I stayed home with my family on Christmas. I spent a great portion of my day organizing my strategy to get revenge. I wanted to be with him but because of my pride, I felt a need to punish him.

Larry came to see me with a present in his hand the day after Christmas. He walked slowly up to the door and passed me the wrapped package. "Merry Christmas! I brought you a Christmas present."

I took the present hesitantly. "Merry Christmas, Larry! Although yesterday was Christmas, not today."

"Why you are so upset, I offered to take you with me yesterday." "It doesn't matter, it's over between us anyway."

He sighed, "Okay I will leave, keep the present."

He tried to kiss me good night; I quickly turned my head away from him.

"Thank you for the beads; they're pretty."

"You are welcome."

We finally said good night after about thirty-five minutes. I retired early that night; and spent several hours going over Larry's actions. I finally came to the conclusion that Larry is too perplexing, therefore I tried to put him out of my thoughts. I exhaled heavily and thought, *With Larry and Andy out of my life for good, I will have more time for my female friendships.*

Sarah Grayson, one of my friends, and I shared some memorable experiences when we were younger. We became friends in first grade, grew up in the same church, slept over, and attended Sunday school conventions as delegates together. Our families remained close as far back as I can remember. It was fun sleeping over at Sarah's house because she had a large family, which included a daddy. I adopted her daddy as my spiritual daddy, after Daddy Ben passed. He admonished me to study my Bible and also encouraged me to stay faithful to the church.

Sarah and I shared the usual girl talk between Sunday school and worship service. We played many games together in elementary school, and even had a few fights, but soon reconciled our differences. All of the fights surrounded name-calling.

During the 1940's African Americans were deceived into viewing being Black as negative. Whenever Sarah would refer to me as "Black Izona;" I would react by reminding her why her skin was lighter than mine. She would tell the teacher; that got me in trouble, which always led to hitting and pushing.

We both transferred to Martin County Training School during our junior high year. Sarah moved to Martin County to live with relatives. I stayed home and crossed the river each day by paddling a boat until Mom finally upgraded to a motorboat. After crossing the river, I would take the school bus to school. Sarah came home on weekends so we still attended the same church on Sunday. She and I had many classes together and participated in school plays, as well as other school activities. I got acquainted with many teenagers in our new school; many of them became close friends.

Larry still came to visit me every few weeks, but I wouldn't forgive him for not coming to see me on Christmas Day. He made his visits short, because of the cold treatment from me, which reflected unforgiveness. He seemed single-minded about renewing our relationship. I was just as determined to make him keep his distance to pay him back for Christmas Day.

Mrs. Betty Jones, Mom's friend often expressed, "Izona, Larry is going to be your husband, because every time you two break up, you end up together again. Just mark my words."

"We are not getting back together this time. He is too stubborn and selfish."

"Izona it seems as if you both have been guilty of stubbornness."

"I'm sorry Mrs. Jones, Larry made his choice; he will just have to live accordingly. Anyway, at this time it is nice to have time for something else other than a boyfriend."

Mrs. Jones smiled at me, and walked up the steps into church. As I went behind, I thought, *How does she know who is the husband for me?* I became mesmerized momentarily when I noticed Larry scrutinizing me during worship service. After getting control of my emotions I thought, *I'm not going to give in, because he hurt me.*

Larry and I always cared deeply for each other, but we allowed stubbornness and pride to interfere with our relationship. At that time I hadn't sought God's will for a husband. It is always God's will for us to consult him regarding every area of our life.

According to Solomon, "Trust in the Lord with all thine heart: and lean not unto thine own understanding. In all thy ways acknowledge him, and he shall direct thy paths," (Proverbs 3:5-6, KJV).

Although we cared for each other, we felt the need to feed our pride instead of trusting and seeking God about our relationship. Pride opens the door for Satan to gain ground in our lives. It is one of the six things God hates, and Satan wants us to have a haughty disposition. If we had trusted and sought God concerning our relationship, it would have made a positive difference in our lives. We both lived a bucolic lifestyle, but I had a proclivity towards sophistication. Almost a year passed since our relationship ended. He came to my house infrequently, but I still held my position.

Meanwhile, during the fall of my sophomore year in high school, I met Charlie Smith, a returning student, about twenty years old. Charlie had a trade and could afford a nice car, clothes, movies, and dinner. My younger boyfriends rode horses, but I was afraid the horses would throw me off.

It was exciting when Charlie gave my friends and me a ride in his light blue car. Charlie named his car Blue Paradise. I made myself light blue dresses to match Blue Paradise. Charlie and I wore a lot of blue to complement his car. I found Charlie was very attractive especially, because he had a plethora of flattering, pleasurable words. We enjoyed going to drive-in movies with other couples; Mom didn't permit me to single date Charlie.

It was common knowledge that Charlie and I were a couple when we returned to school the fall of our junior year. We attended basketball games, football games, homecoming, and tournaments, and he visited me frequently at my home. A few times Larry came to visit me while Charlie and his friend were at my house; which was an uncomfortable situation. I tried to avoid looking into Larry's eyes, because they revealed that he still cherished what we had during our relationship. Meanwhile, Charlie's elaborated speech overwhelmed me.

Chapter Four

Deception

One Sunday when we were in our junior year in high school, my best friends Sarah and I chatted under the shade tree, as the teenagers did each week.

"Sarah, Charlie wants me to meet his grandmother at her house," I told her.

"With narrow eyes, Sarah responded, I suppose you want my opinion?" "Of course I do. Friends usually share these types of things."

We chuckled, changed the subject, and went inside for morning worship. We never mentioned the invitation to his grandmother's again.

Charlie strolled through my front door for Valentine's Day with a beautiful red and white corsage and chocolate covered cherries

He spoke in a soft voice, almost in a whisper, "This is for you, my darling."

I took the candy and he pinned the corsage to my dress. Sarah and I had corsages alike at school after Valentine's Day. It seemed as if our boyfriends had the same taste in corsages.

During the late winter of our junior year Charlie and I went with our friends Greg and Janet to a basketball tournament together for the weekend, at Turner College in Turner, Alabama. I slept at Alice, my sister's house, since she lived in Turner near the college. Charlie and Greg escorted Janet and me to all the basketball games that weekend. After driving back to Martin County Sunday morning we ate breakfast and dinner out, then went to visit Charlie's mother and some of his friends. Afterwards we went to a drive-in-movie. I spent Sunday night with Janet. We were chilly when we arrived at Janet's after sitting at the drive-in-movie until late that night. She lived with Pearl and John Waters, her grandparents, who were pastors of a small church near their home. Pastor Waters built a fire and prayed for us. Mom didn't object to me sleeping over at Janet's house.

Early spring of our junior year we began to get excited about preparations for prom night. I took the Home Economics course, and planned to make my evening gown. I was excited about going to the prom with Charlie. I promised myself, "We will look real special for this affair."

Soon after the basketball weekend at Alice's house, she moved from Turner, Alabama to Dallas, Michigan. The distance didn't stop me from sharing my excitement with Alice about my first prom.

"Alice, remember Charlie, my boyfriend who came to your house in Turner and took me to the basketball tournament? He invited me to go to the prom with him."

"For real! What did you tell him?"

"Of course I told him yes; we have been going steady for a while now."

"What are you going to wear? Where are you going to buy your dress? There are some nice dress shops in Turner near where I use to live."

Miss Kelly, my Home Economics teacher suggested I make my prom dress as a class project. "Remember the gray suit I wore to church when you were home?"

"Yes, it's a nice suit; where did you buy it?"

"I tailored it as a class project in Miss Kelly's class. I am going to ask Mom for $20.00 for the material for my prom gown. That will be plenty enough money for the material. Miss Kelly can get a discount on sewing supplies at the material store in Turner. She told me to just bring her the money, and she will purchase everything that I need."

"Okay, that's nice. Watch out for the mail; I'm going to send you a surprise."

"Thank you, Alice. Will you please tell me what it is?"

"No, I want you to be surprised when you go to the mailbox."

"Alright. I'll check the mailbox every evening when I get off the school bus."

A few days later I drove the motorboat across White Stone River to check our mailbox. Although we lived in Browns County, near White Stone River, our mailbox was by the highway in Martin County. We could see the mailman from our front porch when he drove by during the winter months after the leaves had fallen from the trees. I rushed to the mailbox that Saturday morning to see what the mailman put into our box. I took the mail out of the box, and examined each letter. Finally, I came to one with my name on it. When I ripped it open, I saw that crisp $20.00 bill.

I ran to the motorboat, got in, and drove fast across the river to show Mom the surprise Alice sent me.

"Look Mom, Alice sent me $20. It's enough for Miss Kelly to buy the material for my evening gown for prom."

"Izona, make sure you thank her for me when you answer her letter, because I really appreciate Alice helping out with these expenses in high school. I am glad Miss Kelly is going to teach you how to sew your own prom dress."

I was so excited and could hardly wait to give Miss Kelly the $20.00 so we could get started on my evening gown. I showed the money to Sue Vaughn, my friend as we worked in the sewing room. We were so excited about getting ready for prom and discussing material for my sewing project.

"Oh! That's nice, Izona. What color are you getting?"

"Sue, I'm thinking light blue will be pretty."

"You sure wear a lot of light blue lately."

"Okay, if you must know Sue, I am trying to match Blue Paradise."

"I figured that was what you were trying to do."

Finally, I reached in to my skirt pocket to give Miss Kelly the $20.00. To my surprise the money wasn't in my pocket. I searched all of my books, notebooks, pockets, and the floor trying to find my money. I reported that it was missing to Miss Kelly. She searched our class, the incoming class, and Sue. Miss Kelly ended the search after she didn't fine the money. I remember warm tears rolled down my cheek when I got up enough nerve to tell Alice my story.

"Alice, the person that took my money has to live with their conscience." There was a pause in the conversation.

"It's a probability that some one that knew you had the money is the guilty person."

"I hate to question Sue's integrity, but she could have given the money to her brother when she ran out to talk to him before the search began. Alice, she is my friend."

"Stop crying Izona, I will send you another $20.00."

"Alice it might not get here in time. Miss Kelly said I need to get her the money this week."

"Okay, I will send you a dress already made."

"Thank you Alice. You are so generous."

I thank God for Alice coming to my rescue again. She sent me a store bought evening gown from Dallas, to replace the one I planned to make myself. It was pretty, but I wanted it to match Blue Paradise. I told the girls in my Home Economics class all about my new pink and white gown. The pink bodice covered white lace and was edged with a white net ruffle. The pink net skirt hung full and moved gracefully with the full netted can can slip. The white net shawl draped over the shoulder. I had white lace gloves, rhinestone necklace and earrings to accent the outfit. I could visualize Charlie and myself dancing across the ballroom floor being the center of attraction. *My outfit is ready all I have to do is wait for prom night,* I thought. Excitement filled our classrooms the closer it got to prom night. We had begun to think about our hairstyle appointments, since prom was only a few weeks away. Charlie came to visit me two weeks before our special night. The evening started out as a typical evening together. We sat, chatted, and held each other close as usual. A little before his visit ended, Charlie gave me a quick kiss on the check and informed me in a real low smooth voice, some disappointing news.

"My Darling, I'm so sorry, I won't be able to take you to your prom, because I have to go to Georgia for some important business that weekend."

"Oh no! Charlie is it possible to change the date of your business trip? This is such a short notice."

He spoke ever softer, "My special darling, I wish I could change this business trip. You know how much I love you, right?"

"Okay, I understand, after all you are a business man. I will miss you." We spent the rest of the evening not too talkative. I had made a lot of preparations for my first special night with my special guy. Alice went out of her way to help me to feel special for my first prom. The idea of staying home on my first prom night deflated my ego. The sad news from Charlie was really overwhelming. He finally kissed me, and we said, good night.

I pondered over the situation a few days, being heavyhearted. There was a war going on in my mind. I had a choice to stay home or go to the prom with just a friend and be sad because Charlie, my special friend, was not going to be there. After a few days I decided, "I am not going to miss my junior prom. After all, this is the only time in my life that I can go to my high school junior prom. I will invite John, my fun loving cousin, because I can usually count on him."

Actually John was Daddy Ben's nephew; to me he was my cousin because his uncle became my step-dad when I was only two years old. I went next door to John's house. I shared my problem with him as usual; we could always talk about anything with each other. I just knew John and I would still have a lot of fun, because we always had fun when we got together. His mother always planned parties for the younger children in the neighborhood when the older youth went out. So we were used to partying together. This was the first formal affair for me, but John had gone to others before.

"John, are you free prom weekend? Charlie, my boyfriend, is going to Georgia that weekend. He can't take me to my prom. I hate to miss my junior prom because I've made a lot of preparations."

"Well, let me check to see what's happening. Is the prom next weekend?"

He slowly turned the pages of his little black notebook before answering me.

"Yes, John, it's next weekend. I know this is short notice, but Charlie told me about his trip just last week."

He finally answered me, "Yes, I am free. I'll be glad to take you to the prom. Will you be able to keep up with me on the dance floor?" he teased.

"Sure I can keep up with you, John. Thank you very much for helping out your favorite cousin. I am in a tight spot, since Charlie learned about his business trip just a few weeks ago."

Still determine to be faithful to Charlie; I continued to make plans to go to the prom with John. John and I discussed what he should wear. I told him to buy me a white corsage with white and pink ribbons to match my evening gown.

Excitement intensified in our classrooms during the next week as we prepared for prom night. We decorated the gym with pastel colors, talked about getting hair appointments and our dates for prom night. All the girls were to wear pastel also. I still was able to experience the excitement in spite of Charlie's business trip. I reasoned *I would have fun with my friends. After all, John will be my escort; we always have fun together.*

Enthusiasm filled our entire junior class as we tried to wait patiently for our big night. Everyone in the junior class seemed really happy the day of the prom. We girls talked about our dates, hairstyles, and outfits. Sarah, however never told me who was her date. Annie, another one of my friends, said she was double dating, but I wasn't sure with whom.

After I arrived home I was too elated about the prom and my new outfit to enjoy my dinner. John seemed excited when I saw him also because he loved to dress formally and he enjoyed a good party.

Chapter Five

Prom

Everything seemed to be working out for the prom in spite of Charlie's trip and someone stealing my money for my evening gown. I reasoned while waiting to dress for prom, *Charlie's kindness and gentleness is good for me; it helps me to overcome the fear from the past abuse. As for the person that stole my money, I tolerate their action without imputing criminality, even though I was deeply hurt.* My trusting nature could not have been more wrong and led to many misfortunes.

When we live a prayerful lifestyle and read our Bible, God will give us insight. We won't be as gullible. We have to realize that deception is not new. Just as Satan used the serpent to deceive Eve, he will use people to deceive each other. Everything is not always what it looks and sounds like.

Keep in mind that according to Paul, "For there are many unruly and vain talkers and deceivers," (Titus 1:10, KJV). True love seeks to please God, and is unselfish.

Deceptive love seeks to please self and do and say whatever it takes to get one's own way.

Everything looked perfect, but I wished Charlie were going to be at the prom. My first big ball was to begin in a few hours. Everything was ready except my hair. John came for me a few hours early to take me back across the river to his house. There his sister styled my hair all over my head in small curls. She also helped me get dressed in my prom outfit at their house, since Mom didn't want me to cross the river in my long evening gown. John was dressing in a black and white outfit in the room across the hall. After John and I finished dressing we came into the living room.

"Izona, you look pretty tonight. That business Charlie is taking care of must be real important," he laughed and changed the subject.

"Thank you John, You look real handsome yourself. Tell your girlfriend I said thanks for letting me borrow you for tonight."

"It's okay, she knows we are just cousins and friends. Come, let me pin this corsage on you."

John's hand shook as he pinned the pink and white corsage on my gown. When he finally finished, I pinned his boutonniere to his jacket. He held his arm out for me, "I can't wait to get you on that dance floor."

"Okay, I'm ready for this prom."

He drove up that long dusty road to Martin County Training School. We arrived early to get used to the atmosphere. I watched each couple as they entered the door. They appeared be to very happy as the band played soft music, which added to the festive mood. Each couple was very attractive, and many greeted each other and introduced their guests.

The atmosphere was perfect, but I thought, *if only Charlie were holding my hand and dancing with me, instead of being in Georgia on a business trip.*

John extended his hand toward me and slightly bowed his head, "May I have this dance?"

I gave him my hand and gracefully stood to my feet. We began to dance. We didn't confine our dancing to each other, but we danced with other people. I felt extra special getting so much attention from the boys. My classmates and the faculty knew John was not my boyfriend. They were aware of the fact that Charlie and I were special friends. With all the dancing, and fellowshipping with friends, I managed to get my mind off Charlie for a long period of time. The band began to play lively music. The couples swung, and spun around all across the ballroom. As John was spinning me around, my white and pink cancan slip made my gown stand out and move gracefully. I felt special.

I noticed Sarah and Annie, two of my friends, weren't at the prom yet with their dates. Sarah had been quiet when we talked about our dates the last few weeks, but Annie expressed her excitement about her date earlier that day at school. It surprised me that they were this late.

John kept me so busy on the dance floor until there wasn't time to worry about Charlie's absence. Finally, the band started to play slow music again; John pulled me closer to him, turned my back toward the front door and kept dancing. He gently push me back just far enough for us to see in each other eyes. He looked toward the door, and mysteriously looked at me. He placed his mouth close to my ear and spoke softly.

"Did you say Charlie went out of town on a business trip and that's why he couldn't take you to prom?"

"Yes, why are you looking at me like that?" He was moving me farther away from the door as we danced, but it was hard to continue to dance and keep my back to the door. He finally turned me around facing the front door, and I got a quick glimpse of a couple just entering. I closed my eyes and opened them again slowly to make sure I was seeing accurately. A beautifully dressed young lady was wearing a sky blue evening gown and matching accessories. I checked out her outfit first, but I wanted to see her escort since she had such a glow on her face. My eyes traveled upward until they reach her face. To my surprise it was Sarah, Annie, and their dates. I noticed Annie and her date's outfits complemented each other before checking out Sarah's mystery date.

I reasoned again, *I wish Charlie were here to enjoy my special night with me.* My eyes started at Sarah's escort feet, and traveled upward past his black suit, white shirt, and black bow tie until our eyes met. A lump seemed to rise up in my throat, my palms got sweaty, and my eyes began to burn from holding back the tears. I wanted to scream. Sarah's date was Charlie.

I felt rejected by people I loved and trusted to love me. When I saw Charlie was Sarah's date for the prom, I wanted to slap his face and pull her hair. But pride and shame wouldn't allow my true feelings to surface. I began to laugh and pose as the life of the party. "Keep dancing, John. I don't care."

A sick feeling was in the pit of my stomach after over hearing Sarah's remarks with a smug look on her face.

"She is just trying to cover up her feelings."

Embarrassment, anger, humiliation, low self-esteem, rejection, and deep hurts crowded for attention during prom night. I could have dug a hole in the floor and fell into it until the night was over. I built another wall up around me as a guard to protect myself from ever being hurt again. "John, no one will ever hurt me again."

"Calm down. You will be alright."

"John, I don't want another boyfriend anytime soon; they are more trouble than I need in my life. Whenever I trust one, he does something that causes me pain, so forget it!"

To give me time to come to grips with my shock and disappointment, John danced me all over the gym. I even danced with a few others as I tried to hold myself together. Every now and then I seemed to feel Charlie's eyes fixed on me. When I would look around he was staring in my direction. It must have been the grace of God that helped me through prom night without falling apart. Ned, and some of the other boys from my class tried to be supportive, but I was crushed.

Some of my past experiences left me physically and psychologically wounded. The rejection and betrayal by Charlie and the girls I considered to be my friends left me with depression, distrust, anger, and unforgiveness. When that prom was finally over, the reality hit me that I had misjudged their character. It would not have been so traumatizing if I had only lost Charlie, but I lost the closeness of Sarah and her family. Sarah's dad was the only one in that family that remained close to me. He was a spiritual father figure in my life since I didn't remember my own father. I had overcome many hurts and disappointments in the past and I believed this latest blow would pass. How Charlie handled the situation of preferring to take Sarah to the prom is what seemed so unkind. I was in denial about the extent of my unforgiveness and rejection for many years. Charlie's gentle, and kind ways help to rebuild my trust in men; then he yanked it away by my heartstrings in front of the whole junior and senior class. I built walls of protection around my heart and promised myself, *No one will ever hurt me again.*

The trust I once had in Charlie was gone forever. He wrote me often; I burned the letters on one corner without opening them, and marked in big writing, "RETURN TO THE SENDER." I am not sure what burning the corner meant. Whatever it meant Charlie seemed to ignore the message. He tried to make up with me whenever he got a chance; I couldn't see myself forgiving their actions. My life went in a different direction after prom night. My trust in men was damaged. I decided to put dating on hold for a few years. If you have ever been deceived, lied to, rejected, felt used by a lover and embarrassed, you know how I felt.

You are not alone. Many women and men have had similar experiences and came through it victoriously, or refused to forgive and suffered for many years. My experience was hideous but not unusual. Many women have known someone that they believed would care for them endlessly. We all have been a victim of rejection to some degree by a parent, sibling, boss, friend, housing accommodations, church, the work place, husband or wife. As a result we have experienced depression and insecurity. We confront those feelings by defending ourselves with anger and bitterness.

Suppressed anger can cause one to lash out at innocent people. Our happiness depends on how we handle rejection. If we keep our feelings inside, go into denial by pretending we don't care; we are deceiving ourselves. Anytime someone does something to cause another person to feel unwanted or unloved, it is a form of rejection. Rejection can affect us for a lifetime if we fail to deal with it properly. It can even cause us to fear moving on with other relationships. Remember, our worth is not measured by what some person may say or do to us. God made us in his own image to glorify Him, in short, to move on from jilt to God's Joy.

We need to admit what we are feeling, then decide how Jesus would handle the situation. He would forgive. We all have sinned. Think about the people we might have hurt and seek forgiveness. Jesus is our role model. He wants us to copy Him. He only did what His father said do. He was rejected while on earth. Many reject Him today, yet he loves us unconditionally. Even on the cross Jesus asked Father God to forgive his offenders.

You too can overcome your hurts if you make a choice to set the person free that offended you. Sometimes we try to hold the person in bondage that hurt us by not forgiving them, but in reality we are keeping ourselves in bondage. Much freedom comes to us when we forgive others. I felt justified in holding ill feelings toward my deceivers because of the embarrassment, hurt, and disappointment I experienced in the presence of all my classmates. I didn't know how to deal with such shock. As a result I faked having fun to keep from revealing how really deep I was hurting. Due to pride and shame, I held my hurt in for many years.

When we finally admit our true feeling to ourselves, and God, and forgive the offenders, then healing will began. Healing won't come as long as we try to hold others in bondage through unforgiveness.

If you are holding on to old hurts, it will help set you free if you choose to forgive and move on with your life. If you want to be free, and praise God with a clean heart, pray this prayer.

Dear Heavenly Father,
I have made a choice to forgive and set _____ free. Please forgive me for my sin of holding on to hate, anger, unforgiveness, and pride for so long. Come into my heart,

Jesus, and be Lord of my life. Father God, please forgive my perpetrators and set them free in Jesus' name. Amen.

If this prayer doesn't express the desire of your heart, put one in your own words. Then trust God to start a deep inner healing work in you. Jesus loves each one of us and cares about our hurts. He knows all about rejection and hurts. He understands ours. Trust Jesus because he loves us, and cares about every area of our lives. Regardless of what situations we are in, just remember, "This too shall pass."

"Commit thy ways unto the Lord, trust also in him; and he shall bring it to pass," (Psalms 37:5, KJV). Trust our lives in the Lord's hand for safekeeping. Trust him to heal your hurts and broken hearts, and he shall help this to pass from you.

Chapter Six

Traumatized

I buried myself in schoolwork, sporting events, reading, writing, listening to music, and attending church socials, instead of dealing with my disappointments about Charlie, Sarah, and others that hurt me. I enjoyed corresponding with several pen pals during the summer of 1954. The summer seemed to have gone by fast. I didn't want to be bothered with boyfriends after my prom night experience, so I spent time visiting relatives in nearby towns. Every few weeks some relative would come visit us and take me home with them for a few days. This was a rewarding experience since I lived in a rural area. My uncle took me to spend two weeks with his family, in Birmingham about 100 miles from our home.

But still determined not to get hurt again I continued to build a wall of protection about me. I met a few guys that summer, but since my trust was so shattered I didn't allow myself to get emotionally involved. I made sure I kept them at a distance. I drew a mental line and dared any guy to cross over and get too close to me. I held true to my decision for over a year.

Remember Larry, my childhood sweetheart? During the fall of my senior year he came by to see me and invited me to a movie and dinner. At that time I forgave him for not coming to see me on Christmas Day. I realized then that my love for Larry was genuine. This time he had a car instead of a horse. He kept visiting me occasionally, hoping we could get back together.

Larry came to see me a few weeks before Christmas and surprised me "Izona, I love you, and want you to be my wife."

"I have to finish high school and go to college. Marriage is something that can wait until I'm in my mid-twenties" I told him.

We soon ended the talk about marriage. I wasn't ready for anything that serious. I could tell Larry loved children because of the way he responded to my nieces and nephews. He always gave them a lot of attention. *It's good that he likes these children; I love them also, but I'm not ready for any of my own.* He took me to a few of his school functions and to visit his parents at their home. He didn't mention marriage again. We maintained our friendship. I still didn't have a boyfriend, and I was pleased with that. I kept busy with my senior high school studies, and made sure I didn't get hurt again.

In January Larry moved to Waukegan, Illinois. We kept in touch by writing occasionally, because I didn't have access to a telephone. He found a job three days after arriving at his new destination.

During my teenage years, Mom battled health problems. She went to the hospital in March 1955 for surgery. My sister Alice came home to be with her at the hospital during surgery so I didn't have to miss school. I took care of Alice and Frances' children while Mom was ill. My nieces and nephews attended elementary school all day while I attended high school.

My heart felt sick with dread, I wrung my hands, and chills went down my spine when I got a call at school from the hospital. Some relief came when I heard Alice's voice on the phone saying that Mom came through her surgery well but was in some pain.

I thanked Alice and was able to return to class at ease since she assured me of Mom's condition. Mom came home from the hospital but had to return every few weeks for treatments. After a few weeks Alice returned home to be with her husband in Michigan.

Mom often showed pictures of angels that were in Christian magazines to her grandchildren during her recuperation. She would say to her grandchildren, "Children, this is what Mama will be soon." They would look confused about what she meant, since she gave no further information about the picture or her transformation. I really didn't think too much about the pictures because she was always reading something from the Bible and Christian books. Anyway I was excited about my new hobby of baking and decorating cakes. I made one for her birthday and said, "Mom, I will bake you cakes often now that I have learned this skill in my Home Economic class."

She didn't spend much time on the topic of her own birthday, which was December 25th. With her face glowing, she looked at me with love then raised her eyes heavenward, "Oh, Child, by the time my next birthday comes I will be flying with the cherubim."

I held my head to one side and shrugged my shoulders, as I continued to set the table for her birthday celebration. I was thinking as we ate our Christmas dinner and her birthday cake, *when I finish school and get a good job I will be able to buy Mom nice gifts.* She deserved all I could do for her and more. She shared the story of Jesus Christ's birth with us. This is the only time I can remember us stressing a cake for Mom's birthday. The Christmas spirit usually overwhelmed us so we neglected her birthday.

Just for the sake of conversation I said, "Mom, Larry asked me to marry him."

She didn't seem too excited about the idea, but she finally said, "Izona please ask Larry if he will let you stay here with me a little while longer?"

I was a little bewildered when she said that because she was getting better every day. I told her I had been accepted to a college and wanted to finish college before I get married to anybody. I was just sharing with her what Larry and I discussed when we saw each other last.

During a pause in our conversation someone came to the door. "Mom a man is here taking a survey to see who will sign up for electricity in our area. He said all of our neighbors are signing. May we please sign?"

"No, we won't need it, you'll be living in Dallas with Alice this fall."

"Oh! Are we moving to Dallas?"

"No, I'm not. You and the children are moving to Dallas, I will be flying from glory to glory."

Mom never could hold a tune when singing, but I can still hear her hum the tune of an old spiritual hymn. "Walk--with me-e - Lord—Walk with me. In my trials, walk—with me." She also hummed as she walked through that old country house, with out stretched hands looking toward heaven. "Precious Lord, Take My Hand and Lead Me On."

During the summer of 1955, after my graduation, Mom spent a lot of time telling me so much about the Bible and life. "Izona, whoever you get married to don't be yoked with an unbeliever. If you do, it will cause you to have a hard life. Never marry a gambler, because that can cause heartaches."

In the early part of September Mom and I were washing clothes out under a shade tree when she said "I wish I had some real quiet place where I can go and pray like I want to these last few days."

Maybe I just didn't want to face facts; she tried to prepare me for the sad future, but I blocked out the clues she gave. Finally the first Tuesday in September, Ned drove her to the hospital for treatments. I stayed home with my nieces and nephews. Thursday night I had a dream. I saw Mom get into a bed with real white sheets; they were so bright I needed to squint my eyes. She got in between the two sheets with my dad, who died when I was only six months old. They covered their heads. I didn't dwell on the dream too much during the next day.

Ned left early Friday morning to bring Mom home. It was a beautiful sunny day; and I looked forward to Mom coming home. It had been six months since she spent the night in the hospital. I missed her. We had become very close; we talked about so many things lately. She even talked about the facts of life. She told me about how a mother can feel the baby kicking during the latter months of pregnancy. It seemed as if she was racing, trying to make up for lost time when she talked to me lately. Ned returned home sooner than expected.

"Ned, Where is Mom?"

"Izona, come with me to the hospital if you want to see Mom alive."

"Okay Ned, I want to be there; I have so much to say to her."

I thought, *if I get there in time maybe she wouldn't leave me.*

We gathered her six grandchildren that lived with us. Ned sped all the way to the hospital, but when we got there it was too late; they already had taken her to the morgue. That Saturday the church bell rang with such a lonesome sound to inform neighbors of a death in the area. Wedding bells rang as Charlie, and Sarah took their vows. Traumatic situations seemed to overlap each other. Mom died on Friday, Sarah, my friend, and Charlie, my ex-boyfriend, got married on Saturday, the same weekend. When I really needed friends and church family, the wedding seemed to take everybody's attention. I had lost Mom, Charlie, Sarah, and her family. By keeping my true feelings to myself, most of the neighbors probably thought I just mourned the lost of Mom. No one in my family got an invitation to the wedding. Knowing my true feelings of unforgiveness, hurt, anger, low self-esteem, depression, rejection, on top of all that grief about Mom's death, I probably would have stayed home anyway. If Sarah had sent me an invitation, I might have released all the feelings I had suppressed ever since prom night.

I was lost for words and tears would not come. It seemed as if the weekend would never end. By the time all the family got home from up north to make the funeral arrangements, I almost fell apart. With all the screaming, I went down to the river to jump in to join my parents but these words came to my mind, "Thou shall not kill, and this too shall pass." I thank God for the Word Mom put in me from a young child. The Word came to my rescue in a very needed time. Even though I harbored a lot of ungodly feelings, He was still merciful. It's just like Him to look beyond our faults and see the need. The thought of suicide was a trick of the devil. His reason for coming is to steal, kill, and to destroy.

By the next weekend all of my, siblings, cousins, and friends were home. The Saturday before the funeral Abraham said, "Come on Baby, and view the body."

I wanted to believe this wasn't real. I answered, "No, I don't want to see her."

Ned pleaded with me, "Come on Izona."

"Please leave me alone, Ned, I don't want to go in there."

I walked around bewildered. We crossed the river. A bus was waiting to carry us to church for our mother's funeral. At the church, we lined up and marched in for the funeral service. We three sisters dressed in black dresses made alike. The grandchildren wore navy skirts or pants and white shirts.

I can vaguely remember someone singing, "Precious Lord, take my hand." As people passed by to view the body, my hands felt cold and my knees got weak. Finally my turn came to view my mother's body. I don't really know what happened when I viewed the body. What I remember is someone giving me support at the grave sight. Everything else seemed vague.

The next few months passed quickly as we finished harvesting the crops, selling the household items, farm animals and equipments. My nieces and nephews went to live with their parents in Ohio and Michigan. Ned and I moved to Michigan to live with Alice and her family. The trip to Michigan was intended to be a two-week vacation for me. Then I would spend two weeks with Frances in Ohio, before going to college. I enrolled in a college in Tennessee. Going to a strange college with no home to return to and little money was unsettling.

Alice stated, "Please stay here and go to school in Michigan."

With a sigh of relief, I thought, *I could stay with my sister and her family until I finish college.*

"Okay, Alice I will be glad to stay with you and attend college."

I lived with Alice instead of going to Tennessee, and I avoided dealing with my grief and rejection.

Job was a good example of how to react when we have problems. He lost his children, animals, friends, health and wealth, yet he fell down and worshipped God. Because Job stayed with God and worshipped Him, God brought Job out of his situation victoriously. In the end, God restored to him twice as much as he had before his tragedy. We also can have victory if we praise God in spite of the death or deception by a loved one.

If you have lost someone you loved by death or rejection or have been deceived by people you thought loved you, there is a way to come out victoriously.

Forgive our offenders; forgive yourself for negative reactions. Praise God, pray, read the Word daily, and learn what it says about who you are in God. Thank God for his unchangeable love, because he will never leave you, nor forsake you.

Pray this prayer if you desire to be set free from the result of all the traumatic experiences in your life.

Dear God,
I have been holding on to grief. Please help me to give up my dead loved ones into your care and move on with my life. Holy Spirit, help me to encourage others who have lost loved ones. God help me make a choice to forgive all who have offended me. Help me to put you first, God, others second, and myself last. In Jesus name! Amen.

Chapter Seven

For Better or Worse

A few months after I moved to Michigan to live with Alice, Larry found her telephone number and called me. "Hello Izona, this is Larry. I want to come over to visit you for a weekend real soon."

"Okay Larry. It will be a pleasure to see you. It has been so long since we have seen each other. Don't wait too long. I'm leaving for college in a few weeks."

"Does that mean you are not going to marry me? I love you and want you to be my wife."

"Larry, Mom always wanted me to go to college. It's what I want also."

"If you marry me, I'll send you to college. I have a good job. Please marry me. I promise, you will live like any college graduate."

Larry came over to visit me two weeks later, and his conversation was still about marriage. I was glad to see Larry, but it surprised me that Billy drove him to see me. I felt very uncomfortable in Billy's company. Even though I had suppressed the rape, I didn't like being near him. In fact, it bothered me for someone to mention his name in my presence. I kept the feeling buried deep inside because I thought, *I wouldn't be a good Christian to share those kind of feeling.* I was glad Billy went to visit his relatives while Larry visited me.

I thought about what Mom said about Larry when we were in our mid-teens, "*That boy has a lot of nerve. He doesn't give up too easily, especially about you.*" Whatever I say to him about marriage he had an answer. When the weekend ended Larry drove back home to Illinois.

I pondered over Larry's discussion about marriage. I remembered how kind he seemed during our teen years. He looked out for me during our pre-teen years, and never forced his affection on me as some of the other boys tried to do. I could hear Mrs. Jones' voice saying, "Izona, Larry is your husband. Whoever comes and goes or how many times you break up, you always end up back together."

I thought, *I'm not sure I know what real love means, but I do remember Mom* saying, "*Love will grow.*" All these sayings began to run together in my head.

"*Larry is your husband.*" "*Love will grow.*" "*If you marry me; I will take care of you.*" "*I want to go to college.*" "*I will send you to college.*" "*Please marry me.*"

I reflected on what Mom and Mrs. Jones said as well as what Larry kept saying, and listened to my heart. With calculated grace, I removed the telephone from the stand and dialed the number that Larry had given to me. The telephone rang for a long time before anyone answered. My heart pounded and skin tingled as I waited for Larry to answer the telephone.

His cousin answered the phone. "Hello, may I help you?"

"Yes, Ma'am. May I please speak to Larry? I am his friend from, Michigan."

"Yes you may. Just a minute. I heard her call out, "Larry, telephone. Hurry it is long distance."

I had butterflies in my stomach while I waited for Larry to come on the line. Many things rushed through my mind concerning old hurts, rejection, unforgiveness, shame, guilt, anger, grief, and loneliness. I missed Mom so much and all the people back home in the country.

I finally heard someone pickup the receiver. "Hello."

"Hi Larry, this is Izona. I have been thinking about you a lot lately."

"I can't seem to get you off my mind either. What did you decide, are you going to marry me?"

"Okay Larry, I decided to say yes to your proposal."

Larry spoke with eagerness in his voice, "I will see you Christmas. We can talk further about a wedding date at that time."

Larry came a few days before Christmas. We made plans to be married January 21, 1956. Alice made plans for a big reception for us, after a courthouse marriage. We drove across the state line because Larry and I didn't meet the age requirement to get married in Michigan. Alice and I selected a stunning after-five dress and all the accessories for the reception. Clifford, Alice's husband, and Ned helped shop for the refreshments. We made plans for the reception to be in Alice and Clifford's home, because I didn't have a church home in Dallas.

We sent out invitations to a few of Alice and Clifford's friends, a few relatives we had in Dallas, and to my church back home by way of an announcement. I was somewhat sad about the courthouse marriage and home reception because my dream had been to have a big church wedding with family and friends present. Larry darted over a day early to get his bride. I was only 19 and Larry was 20 years old at that time. Nineteen was old enough for me in the adjacent state, but Larry needed to be twenty-one. When we arrived at the courthouse the clerk gave us some papers to fill out and sign. Larry wanted to make sure he didn't have to show identification, by saying he was 23. I wrote my true age.

The judge stared at the Dallas address and said, "I am tired of these Michigan girls coming across the state line to get married without their parent's consent."

I hyperventilated as I spoke in a low trembling voice, "Your Honor, I don't have any parents."

"Judge, I am her sister. I'll sign for her."

"Okay, are you her guardian?"

"Yes, I am."

"Do you have your court papers to prove you are her legal guardian?"

"No sir."

Alice was trying to help me out as usually, but this time it didn't work.

"Go to court and get guardianship and come back with the proof later. Next case," stated the judge.

The judge's decision dampened our spirits. The wedding reception was scheduled for seven o'clock the same evening.

With raised hands Alice held each side of her head, "What are we going to do? All of our friends are getting ready for the party tonight. It's too late to cancel now."

"Girls can get married in Illinois at eighteen; we can get married there Monday," stated Larry.

"Make sure you two get married Monday. I don't know what Abraham will say if he finds out that I'm letting you go with Larry without being married," expressed Alice.

Dragging my feet, I went along with this idea.
I managed to get through the reception without anyone else finding out we didn't get married. The first night

with Larry passed, but my guilty feeling increased.

Clifford and Alice drove Larry and me to Illinois early the next day. I kept quiet during the long trip. I thought, w*hat if Larry is tricking me about marriage tomorrow. I wanted a church wedding. What if we still can't get married?"*

We finally arrived on Maple Street where we started our lives together. My heart seemed to slump; blood rushed to my face; I broke out in a cold sweat when Alice and Clifford drove off toward their home. I didn't like the area where Larry lived and for the first time I was away from Ned, Alice, and her family since Mom's death. Larry and I began our lives together as husband and wife, but I became conscience-stricken every time someone referred to me as Larry's wife. Time seemed to stand still as we waited to go to the courthouse to get married. A week had gone by already, and Larry hadn't taken off work so we could go get married. Our first payday was on our first Friday together. Larry charged into our bedroom with three strange looking guys and Billy. "Larry what are you doing? I'm ironing in here."

It seemed like Billy came to our house every few days for Larry to go somewhere with him. I resented their relationship. What Billy wanted Larry to do seemed to surmount what I wanted. Billy always told jokes about his activities, that showed disregard for men's and God's law.

He elevated his hands with his palms expanded and quickly moved them backward past his thighs as he charged his way past me, "Go to h---, and get out of my way."

Larry and his friends set in motion in our bedroom a card game with money piled upon a table. We shared an apartment with two other couples. They shared the living room as sleeping quarters. Larry and I occupied the bedroom. By this time I was even more uncomfortable with this whole arrangement. When Larry started his card game, and spoke to me in that tone, my blood ran cold. It seemed as if I could hear my mother's voice, *Never marry a gambler. Don't be unequally yoked with an unbeliever.*

I had too much pride to admit I had lived in sin for almost a week. I felt trapped between our living together without being married, which went against Mom's teaching about unbelievers and putting my pride aside and going back home to Alice. All this turmoil in my life was overwhelming. This lifestyle went against my home training. I didn't know how to deal with this situation. I dashed out of the bedroom and locked myself in the bathroom. Warm, salty tears rolling down my cheeks, and under my chin as I stood looking in the mirror. My eyes were red and swollen from so much crying.

I could hear the loud noises coming from our bedroom. I thought, *this doesn't seem like the quiet Larry I knew as a teenager. I didn't know him as well as I thought. I am living with a stranger. Who is this person?* I could hear Billy's voice over the rest of the men's voices. Billy had a big influence over Larry.

Larry and his friends stayed in the bedroom for so long, that I thought about cutting my wrist with a razor blade. As that thought went through my head I could almost hear my mother's voice saying, "Thou shall not kill."

Larry's neglecting me for Billy and a card game caused me to feel even more rejection. While they were playing, I could hear four-letter words in almost every sentence. The game finally ended, and they all went out; I was glad to be free of the noise. I reasoned, *Things will change. Besides I am too embarrassed to go back to Dallas after making such a mess of my life. When we get married I will work hard at changing his behavior, then we will be just fine.* I finally stopped crying and prepared for bed.

When Larry came home late that night I tried to reason with him, "Larry, I don't like you gambling. I am afraid you may lose all the money. I have heard sometimes people kill each other when they gamble."

"You don't have to worry; I will leave all the money home except my spending money. I promise not to come back for more money when that is gone."

"I am not comfortable with profanity when you speak with me."

"I am sorry, I will watch what I say in the future." It had been one week since I came to Illinois and we still were not married. I wondered if I had made a mistake.

"We can get married at the courthouse Monday morning. Then we will feel better about the whole situation," Larry assured me.

"Okay, I truly hope so."

We went to the courthouse early Monday morning. My stomach knotted as the judge said, "Next." Larry and I held hands as we made our way in front of the Judge.

"State your names, addresses, places of birth, and ages," stated the Judge.

We gave all the information but saved our age for last. Finally I said I was nineteen. Nineteen-year-olds had no problem getting married in Illinois.

It's a relief that in a few minutes I can stop pretending, I thought.

Larry spoke in a trembling voice, "I'm twenty, and will be twenty-one next August."

"Are your parent here to sign for you?"

"No Sir, judge, they are in Alabama, but it is okay with them for me to get married."

"Come back with a letter with their consent. Next."

"What are we going to do Larry, we can't get married until you get twenty-one. That is six months from now, I feel trapped."

"Daddy will sign for me to get married."

"But I can't let your people know we are not married already."

"Well, do you want to go back to Dallas until I get twenty-one?"

I was filled with guilt as I tried to decide what was the better of two evils: Go back to Dallas, and admit we lived together for one and a half weeks under false pretense, or keep living together pretending we are married already until his 21st birthday.

"What if I'm pregnant? We have no other choice. We have to write that letter for consent."

In the letter I begged his dad not to tell Larry's mother we didn't get married one and a half weeks ago. I had too much pride and shame to let her know the truth, so I tried to hide my sins.

We received the consent in a few days from Mr. Clark. Larry and I rushed to the courthouse the next day to take our vows before the judge for better or worse. Things got much worse before they got better. After we were married I thought of something else to worry about. *What if someone that knows us sees the announcement in the newspaper?"* Since I grew up in a strict Christian home, I didn't want anyone else to know that we lived together a few weeks before marriage. In a state of confusion and pride, I was more concerned about what other people thought of me than about pleasing God. Mom taught me to be proud, so I tried to hide my shortcomings from people. Since we didn't put God first in our relationship and with Billy controlling Larry, things got much worse before they got better. Billy was in-and-out of a lot of relationships, marrying some and just staying with some of them. He had children by a lot of different women.

I told Larry that Daddy always said, "Birds of the same feather always flock together." Larry claimed that hanging around with Billy who was in trouble a lot wouldn't bother him. I didn't mention Billy to him again at that time.

According to Solomon, "He that covereth his sins shall not prosper: but whosoever confesseth and forsakes them shall have mercy," (Proverbs 28:13, KJV).

In order for anyone to be blessed of God, one must admit they are not living according to God's law, and repent. God has set his laws. He means for us to follow them without exception. God has a plan for our lives. Only his plan will be pleasing to Him. When we make a mess of our lives, God is always faithful. He rescues us when we confess our sins and repent. If you are guilty of trying to fix your life yourself, and keep making a mess, God will help you. You might have gotten married before getting delivered from past hurts, unforgiveness, and rejection. If any of this is true with you, it is important to establish a prayerful relationship with God. Then you can establish a meaningful relationship with another person.

A right relationship with God will give us peace that surpasses all understanding. Then couples can truly say to each other, "For better or worse." But it takes the love of God in our lives for us to have unconditional love for others. With unconditional love, we can look beyond others faults and see the need. If you have tried many things that didn't work to your advantage, then try Jesus.

Pray this prayer if it expresses the desire of your heart.

Dear God,
Please forgive me for all of my sins. Come into my life Jesus, and be Lord of my life. Fill me with your Holy Spirit, and give me a desire to obey your word. Amen.

If this prayer doesn't express the desire of your heart, put a prayer in your own words. Amen.

Chapter Eight

Misconception

We had been married almost a month when the smell of bacon cooking made me sick. This sickness took my mind off the difficulty we experienced trying to get married without parental consent. Larry took me to a doctor. He confirmed that I was pregnant. We were excited about the baby. I hoped the baby would fill the void in my life since Mom's death. Larry made sure we had the money to get what we needed and wanted within reason.

Larry and I had very different convictions. I had a problem dealing with his cursing which caused my spirit of rejection to go on a rampage. He would look at me in a state of perplexity when I reacted to past rejections and I thought, *if he loved me he wouldn't say that.* I would remember all of my past hurts, try to share some of them, but he would accuse me of blaming him. We both were quite selfish and didn't understand each other's love language. My love language was tenderness, special table setting, a quiet meal at home, and quality time together. Larry's love language was working hard, providing for the family, and buying nice things. I wanted Larry to meet my needs, but at that stage in my life I didn't understand my own needs. Larry didn't realize that since he got married his responsibility was for his family, not Billy. My conscience bothered me because we hadn't been to church since we got married. One Sunday morning I started walking trying to find a church. I went in the first church I saw.

Some of the ladies must have noticed the distressed look on my face. "You must be looking for a specific church. One is across the street; we don't wear lipstick in this church."

I really wanted help for my sin sick soul. I went to a big church across the street. Nobody seemed to notice my presence. I left church feeling worse because I felt rejection from both congregations. As I walked home from church I decided to mention to Larry what the Bible says about profanity and taking God's name in vain. Later that afternoon I stated, "Larry, Mom said, 'we should treat others the way we want to be treated.'"

"That doesn't make her right."

"Larry she is saying what the Bible says because it is our guide."

"Why bring the Bible into this?"

I gave up on that conversation and began cooking dinner. I cooked all foods that he didn't like for the evening meal. We had plenty of verbal fights as I quoted scriptures to him. My life was full of hurt, anger, rejection, bitterness, unforgiveness, and resentment. I allowed my prayer life to diminish. A root of bitterness and a spirit of unforgiveness took up resident in my heart. And Billy was still in and out of our house using profanity when he wasn't in jail .

Problems kept accumulating for Larry and me. In addition to the relationship problem, Larry's job had a big lay-off a few months after we got married, and he was included. He did different odd jobs during the lay-off, and we managed to survive, although some of the jobs didn't pay much money. Larry kept food for the family, paid rent, and utilities on time. We also paid our medical bills and saved a few dollars. We were too busy struggling to manage our money that we didn't have time for verbal fights about personal problems anymore. We got our minds off of ourselves, and agreed on what was best for our family's financial situation.

Twenty months had passed since the big lay-off with no insurance on the odd jobs. By this time we were expecting the second child, and pressure on Larry had grown. He decided to have a talk with his boss about his situation, hoping for an increase in pay knowing we faced another hospital bill without insurance.

According to Larry, he courageously walked into Mr. Speed's office. "Mr. Speed, may I speak with you for a few minutes please?"

"Yes, how can I help you?"

"I have one child, and we are expecting the second one in a few months. I need a raise or I am going to quit, its just that simple."

"Larry, I hate to see you go; you are such a good worker. You are always on time; I can rely on you. I hate to see you go, but, bye."

Larry came home with red eyes. With his head down, he went straight to the bedroom, and fell across the bed. He spoke in so low a tone I could barely hear him. I had never seen him this way before.

"Izona, I don't have a job. I asked for more money. I can't believe he let me go that easily."

"I am sorry. You can find something else. You always have in the past. We are going to be just fine. Watch and see. Oh, by the way, you have some mail."

"Just open it, I don't feel like reading it now."

"Okay." After noticing the letter came from his main job, I opened it eagerly, "It's your call back to work."

He got called back to work one year and eight months after the big lay-off. Larry got up off the bed with excitement and we hugged each other; he picked up Emily, our daughter and kissed her. Joyful tears rolled down our faces, as we overcame another catastrophe in our lives.

With a jubilant expression Larry finally spoke, "The pressure of having another baby without insurance will let up now that I'm going back to work."

"Larry, I am sure everything will work out just fine with good benefits and more money."

We started looking for a roomier apartment and bought all of the usual things for the arrival of our new baby after a few paydays. Finally it seemed as though our relationship had reached fulfillment. The possibility of having a baby boy thrilled us.

We wanted to share the happiness, so we made plans to treat Mrs. Clark, Larry's mother, to a vacation the next summer to meet her grandchildren. I kept busy taking care of our daughter and preparing meals. Larry enjoyed playing with Emily when he got home from work. When he entered the door, she would make a few steps, fall, get up, raise her arms, and say, "Dada." His face glowed as he hugged and kissed her. It was a pleasure to watch Larry and Emily bond. He enjoyed her baby noises.

Some of our acquaintances began to suggest, "Izona, you should get out sometime so you can see what's happening."

"I have plenty to do at home; a woman's work is never done," I would reply. I continued to take care of my responsibilities at home because I was content with my family. I had accepted the fact that Larry enjoyed going out in the evening to enjoy a game of pool, cards, and a beer with Billy and other friends, therefore the fights had ended. I thought, *peace at last.*

I had reached satisfaction with my married life. Larry and I became the proud parent of our first little baby boy 19 months after Emily's birth. We arrived home from the hospital all filled with excitement about our son. A few hours later chaos began. Larry went to the store for a few items we needed for the children. I was cuddling Randy, our son, trying to let Emily get used to her brother when the telephone rung.

"Hello, may I help you?"

"Yes, is Larry home? This is his daddy."

"No, he went to the store for something for the children. We just got home from the hospital with our new son."

"His mother fell dead in the field today," Mr. Clark bluntly stated.

I dreaded telling Larry that news, because I understood the grief of a mother's death. With our son just one week old, I couldn't go to Alabama with him to the funeral.

"Larry made arrangements to go to his mother's funeral. A friend of my family and Larry's stayed with the children and me until he returned home.

This friend was like a big sister to me during my pregnancy. My own sisters lived so far away. She was helpful to me. I would call her when something happen that I didn't understand since she had more experience with parenthood than me. She would tell me when I should call a doctor. Even when I was a little girl, she would fix my hair ribbons and tie my sash when they came too loose at church. I trusted her to tell me what was right.

While Larry was away, she talked to me with compassion. She kept reminding me that regardless of what people were saying about Larry, my lights and phone have never been disconnected. You always have a decent place to live. He must be taking care of home. She also told me that the woman that bumped into me several times and stepped on my foot during my pregnancy with my son was having an affair with Larry. She also told me that this woman got into a fight with another woman over him. I tried not to believe her. But I remembered a few times the woman even threaten me with a knife she carried in her brassiere. She would intimidate me when I started to go to parties with my cousin. Larry would be out playing cards with Billy and other friends. I had so much fear. Someone even called and threaten my life on the phone.

I didn't tell Larry about the threats, since she claimed that she couldn't stand me because I appeared to be so much in Sunday school as a teenager. I was so naïve that I credited her actions to whatever she was drinking at the parties. I noticed that most people acted a little different after a few drinks. After listening to all that my friend told me and remembering all these other incidents, I decided I must confront Larry.

I was upset when he returned home from the funeral. I grieved with him about his mother's death, yet I had to confront him about his action. With veins throbbing at my temple, my voice ascending to a murderous falsetto. I spit out the words with contempt. "Larry, I know what you've been up to when you go to play pool and cards."

"What are you talking about?"

"You know you are guilty of cheating, Larry."

"I'm leaving you, Larry."

After denying his action he said, "You better not take my children."

There was quietness in the room. He finally calmed down and I built up unforgiveness, and walls to protect myself from further hurts. After a few hours of my not talking to him, he decided to go out. This was too much trauma. I needed some quietness as I tried to think.

"I'm going on Maple Street to shoot a few games of pool." *I'm going to protect myself,* I thought. I headed for Maple Street with Larry's gun in my pocket. With my eyes blazing murderously. I remembered Daddy Ben words.

"You are going to be a murderer before you are twenty-one."

As I walked through the dark streets, I could feel myself drifting too far away from my training. It seemed as if I could hear these words, "Thou shall not kill."

I remembered growing up without a father and wondered what would happen to my children if I didn't control myself. I held my head with both hands and said, *"Oh my children are home alone."* I turned around and went home to check on my children. I found them sleeping peacefully. I thought about my options: Put Larry out of the house, and raise two small children without a father in the home. See if Alice would let me come back with her family. Stay with Larry, even though trust and respect has diminished. Believe he is telling the truth when he denied his infidelity.

He uttered, "That woman is just trying to break us up, Izona. She is not your friend. I take good care of my family. Please don't leave me and take my children. I love you, and don't want to lose my family."

I decided to take what seemed to be the easiest way in this situation. At that point in my life it wasn't easy knowing whom to trust. So many people that I trusted as friends let me down. *Maybe Larry is not guilty. What if this acquaintance is trying to deceive me by trying to break-up our home? After all, she is divorced with five children, and I don't want to be in her position.*

After a few days I decided to give our marriage another chance. We visited a small church in our neighborhood. The people were very friendly, but we didn't get the help we needed. Because of pride and shame, I tried to conceal our problems. I was too embarrassed to let anyone know the hurts and rejection I had experienced. I went to church but had become cold hearted from so many hard knocks in life. Hate, anger, unforgiveness, low self-esteem, rejection, pride, shame, seemed to be getting strongholds on me, and I didn't know how to be free. I quoted the Lord's Prayer each night before going to bed hoping to feel better about our situation. I would say, "God forgive me for my sins," but still had a spirit of rejection and I didn't experienced joy and peace.

I continued to attend Sunday school with my children and read them Bible stories but hadn't learned how to apply the Word of God to my situation, therefore I stayed in bondage. My prayer was, "God make Larry holy." But I wanted to hold him in bondage by not forgiving him.

According Solomon, "Trust in the Lord with all thine heart; and lean not unto thine own understanding. In all thy ways acknowledge him, and he shall direct thy path," (Proverbs 3:5-6, KJV).

If we ask God to give us insight on these verses, then in each situation consider what God would have us do. God will give direction for us to follow.

If a couple would seek God concerning their affairs, there will be less room for misconception. God cares about every area of our lives.

If you are having problems in your relationship, make sure you have done the best that you can to live peaceably. When someone breaks the peace and we react the same as they do, we get on their level and feed their evil spirit. Not everyone wants to live peaceably. That's probably why Paul wrote,
"If it be possible, as much as lieth in you, live peaceably with all men," (Romans 12:18, KJV)."

If there is someone with whom you are having trouble living peacefully, then pray this prayer and put that person's name in the blank.

Heavenly Father,
Please let me know what you want me to do to live at peace with _____. Give us the mind to submit our relationship to you, God. Put a willingness in us to pray and read the scripture together daily. Most of all give me to be at peace with you, God. Amen.

Chapter Nine

Empty Vessel

My family was comfortable with the small church in our neighborhood, even though I had strayed from my Christian upbringing. It troubled me sometimes to not live in a Christian home because I accepted Jesus Christ at age twelve and received the water baptism. It takes the spirit of God to draw us to Christ; the baptism (filling) of the Holy Spirit gives us power to live according to God's will. In my early adult life I relapsed into error or sin.

According to St. Mark, a backslider is worse than before he or she got saved. In other words, when a demon leaves a person, and comes back; if he finds him void of the Holy Spirit, he re-enters, bringing seven worse demons with him. That explains why some people do things after they accept Christ and backslide that they wouldn't do before salvation. If someone has known God's love and gone back into sin, Satan will try to drive that person to a point of no return.

I allowed myself to react to others instead of responding according to the Word of God. However, God deals with others' actions, but he takes care of our reaction. When we take matters into our own hands instead of waiting for God's timing, we cause ourselves a lot of heartaches.

I came to the conclusion that Larry might have been innocent of infidelity. A few months later the woman told me he was unfaithful, I heard a knock on our door. A man with a shiny badge on his uniform and a serious look on his face had some papers in his hand for Larry.

"Hello, may I help you?"

"Yes, is Mr. Larry Clark home?"

My knees got weak, salty sweat rolled down my face onto my chapped lips; my hands began to tremble as I responded, "I'm Mrs. Clark, may I help you?"

"No, I need to speak with your husband."

By this time Larry had come to the door. He broke out in a cold sweat, and seemed on edge with a stressed out look on his face as the police spoke to him. He summoned Larry to appear in court. My eyes raking him over with veins throbbing at the temple, as I muttered impatiently. "What's going on here, Larry?"

"I will talk to you later."

My eyes widened, head spun, as the police took my husband to jail. I spent the time walking back and forth during those few hours Larry was at the police station. The children were unsettled also, and I was so conscience-stricken that I couldn't meet their needs. A few hours later Larry returned home looking drained of his strength. I ground out the words between clenched teeth, "Larry, what is all this about?"

"That man took me to jail for a statement."

"But why, Larry?"

"This girl pretends I got her pregnant, but it's not true. A witness will testify to her activities with him."

The witness was Billy. Billy was willing to go to court to help Larry cover his wrong. I wondered, *why would anyone want to take Billy's word since he was in-and-out of jail most of his life.* Billy didn't have much regard for God's law nor men's. He definitely didn't respect women and girls' rights. He believed in earning money the fast way, regardless of who got hurt in the process. After refreshing my memory of Billy's character, I gave Larry a keep-your-mouth-shut look, and spit out words with contempt, "Never touch me again."

Up went the protective walls again. I was at the end of rationality. I thought, *all of this has to come to some type of an end. I can't take anymore. Maybe I will be better off dead. No one cares about me.*

During that depressed moment, I washed down a tonic as strong as a bull, hoping to put an end to my suffering. That wrong decision materialized in a most unpleasing way. With uncontrollable shaking all over, weaken knees, face moist from sweat, palms sweating, head spinning, dryness of mouth, and tears rolling down my cheeks, I thought, *My God, what have I done?* When I came to my senses, I struggled to put the past few minutes out of my memory. I sensed a change had taken place in my body that was nonreversible. I passed a small mass, and later came to the conclusion that I must have been pregnant and what I drank caused it to pass. Satan tricked me into trying to calm my spirit and mind, but this hideous action gave me one more cause to hold on to unforgiveness and guilt. This time I directed it toward myself. There was so much confusion going on in my life during those days until thinking logical was almost impossible.

When the court date appeared, Larry and Billy went to the hearing, but the plaintiff didn't come to the hearing and later put the child up for adoption. Billy's sister adopted the child. Since she took the child, it was easier for Larry and Billy to try to make their claim stick. Larry still tried to convince me that it was a frame-up to break up our marriage. But I knew Billy was willing to help Larry out of any wrong situation, even to say the child might be his.

With so much turmoil in our lives, I called a lawyer and filed for a divorce. I was tired of trying to decide who was telling the truth. At that time, I just wanted out and hoped I would never have to see Larry or Billy again. I gave the lawyer all the information he wanted. He stated, "I will mail the papers to Mr. Clark."

A few days later Larry answered a knock at the door, "Are you Larry Clark?"

"Yes, I am. May I help you?" His eyes widened, hands trembled, and voice cracked, as he read the papers with care. It was a subpoena to appear in court for a divorce. I just wanted out because there must be a better life for my children and me somewhere.

"Izona, please don't leave me. I'm sorry; I promise to do better."

"You can talk to my lawyer. I don't have anything to say to you."

We went to visit the lawyer. He tried to work out dividing our property such as furniture, child support, and visitation.

"She is going to have an apartment in Michigan, and you have to pay her enough to take care of these children."

Larry interrupted, "Sir, she can have all of my paycheck. I can hustle enough for myself." The lawyer gave us counsel, and set a court date. We went home to wait for the court date so this marriage could finally come to an end. There were a few months before the hearing. Meanwhile Larry would get a babysitter and take me out every Friday night.

We would come home and go to our separate rooms to sleep. We did more dating as we waited for the court date for our divorce then before marriage. He shows me a different Larry after I filed for a divorce.

A few weeks before our next appointment with the divorce attorney, Larry had a surprise for me. He suggested that I get my hair done real special. He took me shopping for a new outfit when he got home from work. That night we went to hear a jazz band. The music was soft, lights dim, and Larry introduced me to bubbly wine. As the band played and we sipped our drinks, my mood changed. I became mesmerized looking into those big beautiful brown eyes.

Larry stood up extending his right hand toward me, "May I please have this dance?"

"Yes, I'll dance with you."

We held each other close, with my head resting on his shoulder as we moved rhythmically to the music. I don't recall thinking of his infidelity nor my hideous reaction that night as he shared my bedroom. The next morning all of the anger, unforgiveness, depression, low self-esteem, shame, rejection, and tears returned. I went along pretending everything was all right, all the while planning to go through with the divorce.

At last it was time for us to go for our attorney's visit again. As we sat in the his office he asked, "Have you forgiven him?" I reluctantly looked at him saucer-eyed, lost for words. He rephrased his question, "Have you slept with him?" Quite embarrassed I responded, "Yes, just once."

I actually didn't make a choice to forgive him. I wanted him to suffer for his action. I got so consumed with his action until I just went into denial. *After all I told no one that I didn't really forgive him. My reaction is my business,* I thought.

The attorney scheduled our appointments far apart. I later realized he was trying to allow us time to reconcile. I am glad the lawyer used wisdom by not rushing to grant us a divorce. Before the hearing for the divorce I was pregnant again and I positively had too much pride to get a divorce when I had two small children already. We called off the divorce, went on with our lives, and I became a great pretender. We brought too much excess baggage into our marriage and we were not ready for real commitment.

After I filed for a divorce it was a wake up call for Larry. He spent a lot of time with the children and me during this pregnancy. He worked hard to give us what we needed plus some of our wants. Even though he spent more time with us, I still thought of this woman when he would touch me. This unforgiveness went on for many years and my trust was not restored. Larry moved his dad and siblings in with us, and that didn't help our situation. Larry's dad encouraged him in his street lifestyle by giving him ungodly counsel. Plus, many people in Larry's environment were living ungodly lives. He was deceived into thinking it meant being hen pecked to honor and be faithful to your wife.

I remember one special Sunday morning, with the ground covered with snow and the March wind whistling, Edna, our second daughter, warmed our hearts. We found our children to be very precious. We had two girls and one boy at that time. When Edna was a year old I went to Alabama to my Aunt's funeral. Mom's sister came home to live with me for a while. My father-in-law had remarried and got his own house when my aunt came. She was helpful with our children, the meals, and housework. She reminded me of my mother.

Since I still didn't fully trust Larry to be faithful and I certainly hadn't forgiven him of the past, I felt the need to look out for myself. I enrolled in beauty college so I could earn money and feel independent. My aunt cared for my children until I completed my schooling. She had heard a little about Larry's street lifestyle and would tell me that I didn't have to take Larry's wrong treatments. After attending class for a few weeks, I discovered we were expecting Raymond. I attended class until a few days before Raymond was born. I considered myself blessed because I always desired two boys and two girls. Excitement over our children filled our lives. I thanked God for them and began to tell them about God, although I wasn't faithful to Him myself. Since we lived within walking distance to a church, we started sending the children to Sunday school when we didn't go ourselves, hoping that would justify our wrong.

In addition to Larry's improper behavior, I made a blunder myself in the form of retaliation. I decided to never get hurt again. I looked for happiness in the wrong place. This wrong decision took me a little further than I wanted to go, kept me longer than I wanted to stay, and cost me more than I wanted to pay. It took the power of God to get me out of my entanglement. I am so thankful that God is merciful, that he didn't call Larry and me into judgment while we were living in sin. I always knew where to find my help, even though many times in the past I tried to work things out without God's help and made a big mess. I knew God required me to forgive Larry but I enjoyed keeping him in bondage.

I sought God's forgiveness for my infidelity but held on to anger, depression, unforgiveness, rejection, and low self-esteem. For many years I tried to help other hurting women by placing factual information in their hands. Regardless of the many good works I did, it didn't make restitution for my hidden sins. I often got depressed and angry with myself, and I would find more things to get busy with. For many years I had to be surrounded by others because of so much fear. When I was with a lot of people I didn't have to listen to my conscience. Whatever we have done, God knows. We can hide behind dark glasses but they only hide our eyes from man. God still sees and holds us responsible for all of our actions and reactions. "So then every one of us shall give account of himself to God," (Romans 14:12, KJV).

Because I was void of the Holy Spirit, I did many busy works in church and joined the "right organizations" looking for contentment. I continued to build walls about myself as protection from getting hurt again but I built on a foundation of sand which I discovered could not stand against the schemes of the devil. In order to stand against the devil's plots we need the whole armour of God, according to Ephesians 6:11, 14-17.

Instead of Larry and I putting on the armor of God during our early years of marriage, we donned the helmet of pride and the breastplate of unforgiveness.

Our feet were shod with mischief, and we carried a shield of hatred for ourselves. We had no peace and looked for it in all the wrong places. I found myself in more bondage.

We will not have real peace nor will we prosper when there are hidden sins in our lives according to Solomon. "He that covereth his sins shall not prosper: but whosoever confesseth and forsaketh them shall have mercy," (Proverbs 28:13, KJV). If you too have done something by error or you might have premeditated your action that altered the activities of a fertilized egg it would be better to ask forgiveness. Whatever the reason, God still loves us. He will give us relief of the anger, self-hatred, depression, guilt, fear, and shame. It is far better to face the truth, confess, and seek forgiveness now than wait until judgment day to face God.

Even a tiny mass has everything needed for a human being. Life begins in the mind of God. He knows us at conception. According to David "Behold, I was shaped in iniquity; and in sin did my mother conceive me," (Psalms 51:5, KJV). "For thou hast possessed my reins: thou hast covered me in my mother's womb. I will praise thee; for I am fearfully and wonderfully made: marvelous are thy works; and that my soul knoweth right well. My substance was not hidden from thee, when I was made in secret, and curiously wrought in the lowest parts of the earth. Thine eyes did see my substance," (Psalms 139:13-16a).

According to these scriptures God saw us before we were conceived. God is so awesome. He loves us even when we are void of the Holy Spirit, depressed, half out of our mind, and make improper decisions.

I named my tiny mass that I miscarried and asked her or him for forgiveness. I also asked my family and God for forgiveness. The hard part was to forgive myself for trying to end my suffering, which caused that tiny mass not to reach maturity. I pray that we recognize each other in heaven.

God, please help me make a choice to forgive myself. Amen!

Chapter Ten

Complacent

I became somewhat complacent with my carnal way of living especially when I kept too busy to hear my conscience. I deceived myself by thinking *The Bible states that if we know the will of God and don't do it we will be beaten with many stripes. Maybe I read too much. The more I know, the more I will be responsible for; therefore I will stop reading the Bible so much. That way my punishment may be a little easier.*

I had a great need for acceptance so I acted out of selfish pride. I made sure I attended all the "right" affairs. When I did a few wrongful deeds, I would stay away from church for a few months, than come back and rejoin. That was my way of crying out for help, but nobody heard my cry. Sometimes I prayed, but mostly when I was in trouble.

I deceived myself by thinking, *I'm all right. After all I have nice parties, drink only a little, and listen to my worldly music at home with other church people. Anyway, it's not what you do it is how you do it. There is a right way to do wrong.*

Satan had blinded me. I started to believe his lies. I tried to hold on to the world and God. Then sequence of incidents occurred that caused me to believe God was trying to get my attention. I began to think seriously about my Christian walk. First, I seriously strained my back. I was in and out of the hospital for a year getting treatments. I was under a lot of stress at work and when I took care of our children and our home. Every time I went to the hospital and got bed rest for a few weeks, my back got better, but whenever I returned to work the pain got intense again. The condition triggered panic attacks.

About a year after my back injury Pepper, our dog, got hit by a car. He was special to our family, especially the children. He would walk our oldest daughter to her school, then come back home in time to walk the younger three children to school. One day after the children came home for lunch, Pepper walked them back to school. While he crossed the street to come home, I heard the shrieking of car tires. The shrieking tires, white snow, and Pepper, our black dog is still vivid today after all these years.

Our neighbor screamed, "Oh my God, I have killed those children's dog."

Pepper was knocked 150 feet down the street. Larry and I rushed across and down the street where we found Pepper lying dead in the snow. Tears rolled down our faces as we tried to think of an easy way to break the news to the children.

"Izona, if I take Pepper away it will be easier for them because they won't get to see him wall-eyed and blood running from his mouth and nose."

"Okay, Larry if you think that's the best way to handle the situation."

When they returned home we broke the sad news to them. It broke my heart to see them cry so uncontrollably. They cried out hysterically, and were kicking, and falling down in the snow. Larry had to shake them to get some type of control. After quieting down, they accused Larry of giving Pepper away since they didn't see his body. Then came the third tragedy. Edna, our eleven-year-old daughter was hit by a car, and knocked 200 feet down the street. She was going to a friend's house for a pajama party, but due to her excitement she forgot to look both ways before crossing the street. The car slid from trying to stop quickly on so much snow, but without success. The snow proved to be a blessing; it cushioned the pavement, and Edna suffered only minor injuries. Instead of being killed or badly injured she was only shaken up and frightened.

A few weeks after Edna's accident there was a fourth tragedy. One night, half asleep, I took my pain pills too close together. I fell asleep, but awoke a few minutes later, thinking I had slept for a few hours. I took another dose to ease the severe pain. After realizing how close the doses were to together I became frightened. I called Lawrence, my brother, and he came over within a few minutes to be with me, and called my doctor. My doctor told Lawrence that he would meet us at the hospital at once. He treated me, and after a few hours released me to go home.

I called a few of my friends to complain about my back and the trip to the hospital. I could hear the card games going on in the background, and could tell my friends were having too much fun to listen to my pity party. I stopped feeling sorry for myself, got out of bed, got down on my knees, and called out to God.

"God, I know I have read that you are a healer and I believe the Bible is true. I believe if I pray sincerely you will hear my prayer and answer me. I beg you, please hear my prayer. If you are going to heal my back when I go to the alter Sunday, I want to feel the presence of your Holy Spirit." I got back in bed, and slept peacefully.

The next morning I went to church with my family. The service seemed very special because I felt heat on my back as I kneeled and prayed. I began to praise God. "I thank you, Jesus. I thank you, Jesus." When I went to my seat I felt the presence of God all over me, and my feet wouldn't keep still. When the pastor made the regular altar call for unbelievers or people wanting to join the church, I answered that call. In that congregation it was unusual to answer an altar call if your name was on the roll and you paid your dues. I know now that it's not necessary to ask for signs. God would rather we just believe His word and act in faith. I could hear the usher say to the pastor, "I don't know why Sister Clark is up here. She said she has something to say."

The puzzled look on the usher's face is still vivid in my mind. The pastor looked surprised also. They seemed to think I was all right, since I paid my dues, did a lot of busy work around the church, and was faithful to the congregation, but I needed help. The congregation seemed shocked when I stood at the altar with tears rolling down my face. My lips trembled, and nose ran as the usher passed me some tissue. I wiped my tears away, laid my pride aside, and confessed. "I am a hypocrite. I have worked in the church all these years and not lived up to my confession." I shared all four of the tragedies that occurred so close together in our lives that got my attention. I also told the congregation that I believe God healed my back when we kneeled for prayer earlier that morning.

In the past I would make God a promise. "God, if you help me out of this situation I will serve you." He would help me because He is faithful, and His mercy endures forever. After He helped me through the tragedies, I served Him by attending church often, doing chores, and programs, but still didn't have a relationship with Him. I didn't have real peace because I tried to clean up the outside by improving my conduct. I really desired to do better but held on to so much unforgiveness, rejection, hurt, self-pity, low self-esteem bitterness, and anger that I had a problem controlling my emotions long enough to be steadfast with God. At that time, I didn't know how to deal with all of these negative spirits.

Because I hated my life, I began to pray for God to create in me a clean heart, wash me in the blood of Jesus, put the right spirit in me, and give me a hunger for righteousness, hoping for peace of mind. I knew there must have been more to Christianity than I was experiencing.

When Larry, the children and I next went to Watch Meeting on New Year's Eve, I expected the same service as those held each year. Everyone always said the same thing. But this time my life took a new direction. That night I heard a visitor's testimony about the power of God. I got hungry for that boldness. I asked God to give me something to say and the gift to say it boldly. With butterflies in my stomach I stood to say something like,

"I want to be a better Christian next year than I was last year." Instead unexpected words poured out. "God wants me to teach His Word." I wanted to reach out and take back what I'd said. I wondered why did I say that because I didn't feel qualified to teach the Bible.

"The next day, I told my Christian neighbor of my experience. "I asked God for something to say. 'He wants me to teach the Bible came out of my mouth.' Can you believe that?"

"Yes, it seems like he answered your prayer."

"But I'm afraid to teach the Bible."

"Study. He will help you."

I started attending Sunday school conventions and workshops trying to be a more informed church worker. I hoped to learn a few tips about how to teach Sunday school. Since I was so shy, I would pray to get enough nerve to speak to ten junior high girls. I only taught them what I read in the Bible myself. I would fast and pray often, hoping to crucify the flesh and to hear from God. During this time He started anointing me to expound on the word. I began to love the Word of God.

I continued to pray everyday, "God have mercy on me, create in me a clean heart, renew the right spirit within me, take out the stony heart, and give me a heart of flesh." As I continued to teach Sunday school and study the Word, the scriptures showed me my shortcomings. I prayed for help. Sometimes the Holy Spirit tugged at my heart, but I would desire Him to move back a little. I was afraid to get all the way over on the Lord's side. I believed, *if you get too holy you will die.* Friends also told me, "If you read the Bible too much, you will go crazy."

I thought about this, *if I live as God wants me to live, I would be labeled as crazy.* I began to justify my complacent attitude by saying, "After all we are under grace; therefore God will forgive me if I slow up reading the Bible." The Holy Spirit ministered to me with a scripture in a dream, I knew exactly what it meant, and changed my mind about reading the Bible less. But I was still embarrassed to let my co-teacher know I believed in sanctification, (being set apart, living a clean life) because she was ridiculing others for their belief. Although I wasn't sanctified, I knew in my heart it was right. That night while I prayed, a still inner voice spoke to my spirit, "Psalms 31." As I read it, the words "Let me never be ashamed, deliver me in thy righteousness," seemed to stand out to me. I cried to God, "Please forgive me for being ashamed to admit I believe in sanctification." I meant it from the depth of my heart. I felt truly sorry and desired to live according to the Bible, but didn't want the persecution. After repenting for being ashamed to let my church members know I believed sanctification, I slept comfortable that night.

The next morning during altar call I went down and praised God. He delivered me; I thought everybody was praising God, because the praises seemed to have filled the room. Finally I was free at last of feeling shame for what people thought about my stand for God. I lifted my hands before a holy God and praised Him. David said in the Psalms, "Make a joyful noise unto the Lord." Psalms 146-150 begins and ends with, Praise ye the Lord! Therefore praise is very important to God. After God delivered me from being embarrassed about lifting up my hands and praising Him, my appetite increased for the things of Him.

The world seems to look at us as fools when we don't live worldly anymore. They can't understand believers because they are of another kingdom, a peculiar people. I came to the conclusion that by the world's standards the saved are fools, but by God's standard the one who prepares for this life and does not take care of his soul is a fool. Notice the parable of a certain rich man, in Luke 12:16b-20. It is better to obey God regardless of what people say or think about us. I decided if being peculiar is thought of as being a fool, then I will be a fool for Christ. I still had a problem with what to say when people teased me about trying to be "so holy." The Holy Spirit ministered to me in a dream again. In this dream, I asked, "What should I say when I am referred to as 'so holy?' I heard a voice in my dream, that said, 'Say, I am trying.' That has been my response since that dream.

The next thing I had to deal with was making my stand clear to Larry. I looked him in the eyes and said, "Larry from here on, God is first place in my life. You will have to be second."

His knees got weak, he shook his head, and tears surfaced in his eyes, "What kind of competition is that?"

I continued to look at him with tears in my eyes and said, "This is how I want it and will gladly take second place in your life if you will only put God first. This is what I have to do." I could tell he didn't understand. The state of being a lukewarm Christian had become uncomfortable. There was no more satisfaction with the up-and-down in my walk with God. I settled it in my mind that I was moving closer to God.

God said, "I would thou wert cold or hot. So then because thou art lukewarm, and neither cold nor hot, I will spue thee out of my mouth,"(Revelation 3:15b-16).

Chapter Eleven

Power of Forgiveness

After being tired of a state of complacency, I wanted rest for my weary soul. I went to a workshop on forgiveness. It proved to be a positive experience. I learned that after we forgive someone, anger will not surface when his or her name or the incident is mentioned. I pondered what was being taught and remembered a few people that hurt me in the past.

Even though, I have said, "I forgive you because the Bible says to forgive." I still had plenty of negative reaction when certain incidents would be recalled. My lips would purse with suppressed fury, nostrils flare, and veins in my neck swell. I threw up my hands with disgust as unforgiveness surfaced. Then I remembered the forgiveness workshop.

I could hear the workshop leader's words, "When we forgive, we will not get that funny feeling inside." A funny feeling is putting it mildly compared to what I was experiencing at that time. Let us just say it would have been a dangerous time in my life to die. After searching the scripture looking for help for my soul, I carefully read Matthew the sixth chapter and came to the conclusion that if I didn't forgive, God will not forgive me.

God works within the guidelines of His Word. If we want God to forgive us we must forgive others. If we have a problem forgiving, just make a decision to forgive. When I told God that I was making a choice to forgive, the Holy Ghost, my helper, immediately came to the rescue and helped me with that decision.

According to Matthew 6:12,14,15, "And forgive us our debts, as we forgive our debtors. For if ye forgive men their trespasses, your heavenly Father will also forgive you: But if ye forgive not men their trespasses, neither will your Father forgive your trespasses."

When we have problems forgiving others, we can ask the Holy Spirit to help us to make a decision to forgive. When I decided to forgive, the inner healing was set in motion, but it took time for complete healing. When we walk in obedience to God we are to pray for those who treat us wrong, but it takes godly love to carry out this commandment in sincerity. When someone treats us wrong we sometimes want to penalize him or her by holding on to a hurt for many years without setting the offender free. But the truth is, until we set others free, we will never be free ourselves. A sinner can treat someone nicely who is nice to him or her. It takes the love of God to be nice to those who hate you. It was hard for me to lay aside my pride, love those that hate me, and pray for those who despitefully used me. With tears in my eyes I prayed for my enemies because I wanted God to forgive me of my transgressions. I humbled myself and obeyed the word of God that I may be set free of the disease of unforgiveness. I said, "God, please forgive and bless those that abused, hated, hurt, and used me." In order to obey the Word of God I prayed that prayer daily. After much prayer, one morning I woke and actually desired salvation for those that misused and abused me.

I prayed, "God, those are souls. I plead with you, please save them, because they are blind to the real truth. Please put godly love in my heart for all people," as tears rolled down my cheeks. I have noticed it is hard to hold a grudge or unforgiveness against someone we are seriously praying for. God honors our effort to obey His Word. Finally after a few weeks of praying for those who hurt me the power of God began a work of forgiveness in my heart. I saw them as souls in need of a savior. I see all believers as my sisters and brothers in Christ. At this point in my life I prayed, "God, please, I want to know what is in my heart. Put your spotlight on me that I may know what I should ask you to fix. Let me know whom else I need to forgive." Little by little God revealed some of my old personality that was still concealed. I repented each time He revealed something. We probably couldn't handle it if He revealed everything at one time.

At a revival meeting, I listened to the message about what it will be like when we stand before God on judgment day. I reflected back to when I drank the strong tonic, trying to end my suffering. I shared that experience with several counselors. They prayed for me and assured me that I was forgiven. Since I was so hard on myself, I believed I still had pride. I repented of the pride and shared my secret with my family.

My family forgave me, and Emily helped me to come up with the name, Re'er-hope for the mass I passed. We used the first letters in our other children's names and added HOPE. We thought this would give us the feeling that Re'er-hope is a part of our family. We hope to recognize each other in heaven. I have experienced total forgiveness from God, family, and self. There is no guilt or shame anymore when I remember the incident. That happened during a period of emptiness and despair. I am a new person, living for God, and walking in the Spirit.

For many years before I confessed this secret, I had a desire within me to help hurting women. I tried to do good works, such as helping women to make informed decision during crisis pregnancies. I read many articles and books concerning sexual abuse, rape, premarital sex, and what God says about them. I was looking for answers, but my deliverance came through confession, and repentance. Now that I am delivered, I can inform other hurting women of some of the consequences from reacting under stress. Negative actions during depressed moments can causes great harm. Good action can cause positive repercussion. While trying to help others through doing interviews and research, and soliciting prayers for abused children and their abusers, I discovered a desire to get help for myself. Every time I tried to discuss rape, fullness would rise up in my chest. Finally one afternoon, crying uncontrollable, I became so choked with emotion that I found it hard to speak, much less breathe.

I shared this with Larry; he comforted me and prayed for my inner healing. Now if the need arises, it's not so hard to talk about the rape. There is no need to mention it except for ministry, since I forgave Billy. I inquired about Billy's address because I felt it would complete my inner healing if I let him know that I forgave him for raping me. Billy's sister gave me his address in prison where he was doing time for illegal drug business and rape. I wrote Billy a letter to let him know I forgave him. I never mentioned anything about what he was being forgiven for, but he knew exactly what I meant. After letting him know he was forgiven, I gave him the plan of salvation. A few weeks later a letter came from Billy, addressed to me.

This is his reply. "Izona, I received your letter a few days ago. I hesitated with my reply because I had to sort out my true feelings about such a long ago sin. I was very young and naįve, but that didn't excuse my behavior. Throughout my entire life I have committed sin in one form or another. That is the sole reason for my being where I am today (prison). My sinful past is also cause enough for me to establish a personal relationship with God."

Billy continued, "I believe that it was an urging from God that encouraged you to write me and tell me of your forgiveness of my past sin. I have asked God to forgive me of my sins. The letter from you was like a letter from God. I do believe God will speak to us through other people. Therefore, I took your letter as a sign, too, that if I continue to learn God's Word, trust in Him, and learn His will for me, not only will the remainder of my life be better on earth, but will be ten time greater in heaven."

I was tearful as I continued to read Billy's letter. "I thank you for the letter of forgiveness and the encouragement it gave me to continue seeking God."

I rejoiced for this soul that has been added to the kingdom of God. I want to thank each person that prayed for the inner healing for abused children and their abuser, which I requested in the newsletters I have sent out to two hundred readers for two years. I was one of the abused children. God's grace is amazing. I got inner healing and my abuser got saved. I want to thank you if you are among those who prayed for us.

I returned to my high school for a reunion. To my surprise, many schoolmates remembered and mentioned my prom night experience. Some of them expressed guilt for not being loyal to our friendship. Their disloyalty was not the real problem. Allowing unforgiveness to take up residence in my heart was the real problem. Another incident surprised me when a dear friend shared during a revival meeting that she uses me as an example many times during her teaching. She tells how gracefully I handled prom night. After that I took on guilt for allowing her to continue to believe the prom nigh experience didn't bother me.

Finally I expressed to Sarah and Charlie that I had made a choice to forgive them for the embarrassment and shame I suffered on prom night. Sarah and I embraced each other in love, and that was a glorious reunion for the two of us, but Charlie seemed very uncomfortable.

In the past I had a problem with forgiving Larry for some of his actions. He was expected to make me happy instead of causing me to experience additional rejection. But much of the rejection, hurts, unforgiveness, and low self-esteem were brought into the marriage. We both had excess baggage.

When he would say or do something that hurt my feelings, I would think of many hurts from my past. I finally renounced the spirit of unforgiveness and rejection that I had allowed to take root in my heart. Unforgiveness is a sickness that will destroy our health, and, more serious, our walk with God. We will not go to heaven with unforgiveness in our heart. Unforgiveness can cause health problems.

According to Charles Stanley, "Unforgiveness puts an overload on the nervous system, and eventually, a fuse will blow in some area of your body. The physical body was not designed by God to endure the long-standing stress caused by a spirit of unforgiveness." [2]

This has proven to be true in my life. I carried the load of unforgiveness for so many years, and suffered many illnesses, including nervousness, stress, high blood pressure, and an ulcer. Now that I am walking in forgiveness, my overall health is improved; the ulcer symptoms have been gone for a few years now. Many foods that caused stomach problems in the past don't bother me anymore. Praise God! I am delivered.

My freedom came when I set others free by forgiving them. As long as we hold others in bondage, we cause misery for ourselves. I also discovered that real happiness doesn't have anything to do with other people. It depends on our relationship with God.

"Happy is that people, whose God is the Lord" (Psalms 144:15b, KJV).

Since the inner man is what will go into eternity, I will concentrate on pleasing God by renewing my mind, walking in the Spirit, and making Jesus lord of my life.

Larry and I know more about covenant now than when we took our vows. After taking a Marriage for Life Class, we invited God into our marriage, and prayed that He forgive us. He brought us into a One-Flesh ministry. We praise God for the opportunity to use our negative experiences to help other hurting couples. We know now, without God being head of the marriage and walking in forgiveness and repentance there is no peace. It takes the love of God for anybody to love his wife as Christ loves the Church. In our own strength, we love if or because of others action, but God loves in spite of what we do. It is imperative that we have God in our lives in order to forgive and love everybody. God is love. Our knowing Him enables us to love and forgive others. God will forgive all of our sins if we repent, (become godly sorry), and forsake, (turn away from) them.

"Wherefore I say unto you, All manner of sin and blasphemy shall be forgiven unto men. And whosoever speaketh a word against the Son of man, it shall be forgiven him: but whosoever speaketh against the Holy Ghost, it shall not be forgiven him, neither in this world, neither in the world to come" (Matthew 12:31-32, KJV).

God is merciful, and gives us grace. When He forgives us of our sins, He puts them far from us. It is Satan who reminds us of our sins. He also desires to keep us ashamed and too proud to confess our sins and ask for forgiveness. That hinders us from walking in the anointing and living a victorious life in Christ Jesus. Larry and I were not in a position to love anyone with a pure heart until we forgave each other and I forgave my abusers. Once I started walking in forgiveness, God gave me an inner healing.

My reason for sharing my experiences is to let others know they are not alone in their situation. Whatever your situation maybe, picture Jesus standing with out stretched-arms saying, "Come unto me, I will give you rest. I love you and hung on the rugged cross that you too might be free. I came that you might have life abundantly. Even if your sins are great in man's sight, yet I will wash them white as snow. There is no big sin in my Father's sight. Come to me, my child, that you may live with my Father and me forever."

Accept God's forgiveness; accept Jesus' invitation to come to him; make a decision to forgive others and yourself. He will wash us in His blood by faith, which unifies his people. When we accept Jesus as Lord of our lives, God sees us through His son's shed blood. Through much prayer, being honest about our feelings, seeing a person as God sees them, and walking in forgiveness will knit us together in love. When we know God, instead of just knowing of Him, His love will reflect out of us toward all people. As true Christians we can love each other in spite of our ugly past. When all of God's creation starts walking in the spirit of forgiveness and love, we will complete his beautiful bouquet. Each flower in an arrangement compliments each other. Every race of people has something that the other can benefit from.

If you have unforgiveness in your life toward others or yourself, setting others free can set you free. When we harbor unforgiveness it hurts us more than the other person. We need to make a conscious decision to forgive those that did us wrong, then God will help us with the inner healing. The inner healing starts at the point we let God know that we choose to forgive.

The devil will try to deceive us by means of justifying our unforgiveness. He will bring to our minds *they deserve the negative treatments from you, because of how you were hurt by them.* We have to remember the devil is a liar, the father of lies. God wants us to treat others, as we want them to treat us. If we want God's forgiveness, we must forgive others.

God will forgive us of our sins regardless of how often if we ask Him. There is power and liberty in forgiveness.

Several years after I let Billy know that I forgave him, someone mentioned that he was out of prison and living a saved life. I thought, *that's nice, a*nd didn't think about him or what he was doing with his life. But a few months later Larry and I got a phone call to tell us that Billy had died. For a few days, I did some deep soul searching trying to figure out what I was feeling concerning his death. Someone wanted to know if we were going to Illinois to the funeral. The only thing I was sure of at that time was I didn't want to attend his funeral. Was I glad he got save before he died? Was I glad he died so I will not have to see him again in this life? Or was I allowing anger to return because he raped me many years ago. In the middle of all that emotional turmoil, I tried to carry on small talk with Larry. He just brushed me off and kept glancing at his newspaper that he bought a few minutes earlier. I felt like I would have busted open had I held my feeling inside any longer.

When Larry stopped the car at an intersection on US highway 80. I raised both knees as high as I could get them, put my head back, balled up my fists, and let out three screams as loud as I could. "Gee, that felt good," I said to Larry.

He looked at me as if he was thinking, *what did I do wrong? Why did she scream?* But he never said a word. When we got home I put up a few items we had bought from the grocery store. He sat at the table and began to read the newspaper.

I walked over to the table and said, "Larry, I am going to tell you the reason that I screamed, and I want you to listen."

He could tell I was serious, and wasn't going to settle for a casual half-hearted answer with eyes still on the newspaper.

This is the reason I screamed: I screamed for the little girl whose father died when she was only six month old. I screamed for the young girl that was frightened by older men at an early age.

I screamed for the young girl that a neighbor wanted to sexual abuse.

I screamed for the young teenager that got raped.

I screamed for the young wife that later found out that her husband and Billy was close and he was always coming around.

I screamed for the wife whose husband thought it was hen pecked to stay home with his family, and be faithful to his vows.

I screamed for the wife whose husband loaned Billy our car to drive to Alabama with a group of ladies and insisted that I had to go with them.

I screamed because I later learned that one of the ladies was Billy's girlfriend and the other one yours and she was bring seven children back in a car that already had five adults and two babies.

Larry, I screamed because I needed to let out all of these emotions.

I screamed because I felt guilty for not being able to share your grief.

That scream finally brought closure to my emotional issues concerning Billy. I later repented and decided to forgive and forget.

If you are having problems choosing to forgive, pray this prayer.

Dear God,
I am having trouble experiencing forgiveness and freedom. Holy Spirit, please help me decide to forgive my abusers that I may be free. God, please forgive me for holding on to the sin of unforgiveness. I realize no sin will enter into the kingdom of God, Amen.

Once we forgive someone, what happened to us in the past is not as important any more.

Chapter Twelve

Pursue His Joy

After deciding to forgive, I wanted a personal relationship with God, deep inner peace, and desired to know the voice of God. I began to pray, "God, I want you. I have to know you because you said your sheep know your voice, and will not follow a stranger."

I wanted to be his close friend because a friend sticks closer than a brother. I asked God to reveal Himself to me. When we get revelation knowledge, of who God is, our lives will never be the same. Paul was never the same after he had an encounter with Jesus on route to Damascus. He knew he had met the Lord, because he recognized Jesus' voice as the voice of the Lord. His sight was gone, but he gained insight about Jesus. When we know someone, his or her voice is familiar.

If Larry calls my name along with one hundred other people, even with my eyes closed I would know his voice because I know him. The Holy Spirit is our helper, and we can ask for His help in all things. I asked him to please help me to know God's voice.

After reading Hebrews the eleventh chapter concerning the heroes of faith, I began asking for more power, love, joy, and faith, such as the men and women of the Bible experienced. I went through that faith chapter and saw that each person had great faith. Then I asked God for that type of faith. Hebrews 11:6, states, "He is a rewarder of them that diligently seek him." That phrase touched me in a special way. I reflected on it for a while. *If I diligently seek Him he will reward me.* I became curious about diligently seeking God. The thought of *how to diligently seek him* had become continual.

As I began praying, praising and worshiping God in church during prayer service,

"Diligently seek Him" was still on my mind. I continued to meditate. *To seek is to search, question, try to find something or someone.*

I asked the Holy Spirit to show me how to diligently seek God. After I saw a Strong Concordance there in church, I looked up "diligently seek him" in Greek. Diligently Seek- (Gr.*ekzeteo),* to search out, i.e. (fig.) investigate, crave, demand, (by Heb.) worship – en – (re-) quire, seek after (carefully, diligently).[3] The word "crave" stood out when I read it. I asked the Holy Spirit to put a craving in me for God. I continued to praise God until worship came and a craving for Him came. I prayed, *God, this morning I just want you. In the past I have been asking for your attributes, but today I am just asking for you.* The craving for God intensified in me. I continued to plead with God as a little helpless child wanting something from his or her parent. *I want you God, more than love, joy, and peace; I just want you. God, I have prayed for years for a good relationship with my husband, but my desire for you is greater than that. More than everything being well with my children and grandchildren, I must have you, God.*

Earthly things didn't matter to me anymore; I just wanted God. My thoughts were consumed with seeking God. The craving grew more intense. My entire consecration was on how much I wanted God. Hot tears of desperation humbleness streamed down my cheeks onto my neck as I diligently sought God. My pleading voice took on a hitch of great lamentation, "Please God, I want you. I must have you. I want you more than I want to be a writer, more than I want to teach and proclaim your word. God, I desperately want you more than money, houses and land. I want you more than a degree."

I continued to pray and the craving pulled at my stomach. Sobbing, I elevated my hands, and I knew the seeking wasn't of my own strength. I had no strength left. "God, I want you more than a healed body." By this time the craving for God was so great that I felt as if I couldn't stand it any longer and live.

The Holy Spirit took over. There was no turning back in my seeking Him. I had a craving that surpassed all understanding. The craving within me was greater than anything I ever imagined. If I think of any natural thing that I have had a craving for and multiply it by one hundred I might begin to describe the intensity of the desire for God. The craving became so intense that with raised hand and weakened knees; I surrendered to the craving within me.

On my knees I pleaded helplessness, "God, I want you more than life."

It was then I knew what it means to "diligently seek God." To diligently seek Him is to want Him more than anything else in this world, even more than the ministry gifts, and the fruits of the spirit. According to Galatians 5:22, the fruits of the Spirit are love, joy, peace, longsuffering, gentleness, goodness, faith, Meekness, temperance.

After this experience of diligently seeking Him, I can see more clearly what Paul meant in Philippians 3:7, 8, 10a, "But what things were gain to me, those I counted loss for Christ. Yea doubtless, and I count all things but loss for the excellency of the knowledge of Christ Jesus my Lord: for whom I have suffered the loss of all things, and do count them but dung, that I may win Christ, That I may know him, and the power of his resurrection, and the fellowship of his sufferings," (KJV).

All of the material things that were important to me in the past became insignificant after learning how to diligently seek God. I just wanted to know Christ in a personal way. We must continue to seek him with all of our hearts to receive his promises. To read a book, and tell the high points of the story is good, but it takes on a different meaning when we become personal friends with the author. This is what happens to me with Jesus; I can talk about the Bible with authority now that I sought and found the author. Since He taught me how to diligently seek Him, I gained peace that surpasses all understanding. In fact, for a week after my experience all I desired to pray was, "God, I just want you because you are so good. I magnify you. You are an awesome God. Bless your name, all that is within me, bless your holy name." I didn't want to ask Him for personal things. My desires have changed; pleasing Him is my priority now. I continue to seek Him; I can't get enough of Jesus. The more I seek God the greater the hunger for righteousness become in me. There is a craving in me, and I don't want it to leave. I am a new creature in Christ Jesus. Old things have passed away.

Larry and I get up early in the morning and spend time with our Heavenly Father. I like to pray the Psalms. God puts His approval on our quoting his word to Him in the form of a prayer. I am experiencing greater peace and joy through praying, worshiping, praising God and loving His Word. Speaking what God's Word says about me makes me have a positive outlook about life. I don't experience fear, anger, low self-esteem, shame and guilt; instead I have love, joy, peace, and hope. I know who I am in Christ Jesus. I still seek to know God in a personal way and walk in forgiveness. I have asked Holy Spirit to help me to fall in love with the Word of God because those who love God's Word have great peace.

Okay, just think about if our husbands want us only for what we do for them. How would that make us feel? Then think about how it must make God feel when we only come to Him when we are in trouble or want Him to give us something. He desires us to pray, praise and worship Him, just because we love Him and want to be in His presence. Diligently pursue Him!

I allowed anger, resentment, unforgiveness, and a spirit of rejection, disappointments, fear, low self-esteem, and depression to rob me of joy. I spent many nights lamenting the abuse, rejection, deception of friends, and my mother's death. Sometimes the recurrence of negative experiences was overwhelming. I didn't allow healing to occur before Larry and I took our vows. We both brought baggage, hang-ups, and misconceptions from our past into our marriage, so it was no surprise we experienced infidelity and ended up in divorce court.

Many things we suffered in the past were a direct attack from Satan. We also made wrong decisions while under his influence and suffered the consequences later. I realize that God permits bad things to happen to us because Satan can only do what God allows. God will use these negative experiences in a way that He receives the glory if we love Him. Although Satan meant them for harm, God can use our victorious testimonies to set other hurting people free.

I came through victoriously after turning to God for help. I held myself in bondage by not setting my perpetrators free. Once I made a decision to forgive others; God set me free. When we refuse to forgive others, God will not forgive us of our sins. God has a design for each of our lives from the beginning, but Satan's strategy is to destroy its chances of coming to pass. Satan knows God has chosen us to be holy, and without blame before Him in love. I believe it was predestinated that I, a deeply hurting woman, be set free to help others so Satan tried to cause so much agony to cumulate that I would take my life. When that didn't work, he planned for me to harbor pride, shame, and unforgiveness, and to hide my sins. Pride is one of the six things that God hates. I repented, and stopped hiding my sins in order to prosper. To please God it is important to confess our sins and forsake them.

If Satan doesn't take our lives he will steal our victorious testimonies, joy, and peace of mind. He doesn't want us to walk in forgiveness nor have the anointing because the anointing breaks the yoke in our lives. When the yokes are broken there is a freedom that gives us joy, and peace of mind. The Holy Spirit is our helper, and He will gladly help us to maintain our joy. Just treat Him as a personal friend by keeping an on-going chat with Him.

My prayer life is richer, and I'm experiencing great joy since I started to pray the scriptures. I take a Bible verse, put it in the form of a prayer, and pray it back to God. Praying the scriptures assures me of praying God's will, and He answers. The Holy Spirit is the third person of the godhead and I treat Him as my personal friend. I can ask Him something, and He gives me an answer. I get a joyful feeling when He speaks to me, even when it comes in the form of correction. I know He corrects me because He loves me. After spending a few hours praying in the Spirit, I experience great joy and do warfare by putting the devil under my feet where he belongs. I tell him, "Devil, get out of my family, my house, my business, and me. In fact, get out, and stay out!" I know he gets on the run, because my peace and joy are restored immediately. I am learning the key to a joyful life by praising, worshiping, praying the Psalms, and dancing before God. I ask God to help me fall in love with His Word and put it into practice. As I rejoice His glory comes upon me. I would not trade the joy I am experiencing now for all of the gold in the world. This joy doesn't have anything to do with mankind nor any tangible thing; it comes from God. I pursued his joy and no one can take it away. But we can give up our joy. When someone does something that could steal my joy, I stay focused by leaping, shouting, and praising God. When we get filled with the Holy Spirit, joy comes with it. Satan works hard through others to steal it away from us. Think about this. If Satan succeeds at stealing our joy, we are sad and complaining. His goal is to make the Christian less affective. It works when we let him steal our joy.

Larry and I plan to spend the rest of our lives together thanking and praising God for our blessing: our walk's together, being prayer partners, and being filled with the precious Holy Spirit. We thank God for our family, their love for us, and our love for them. Most of them are in church. We also thank Him that our last years are our best years. Our lives get sweeter and sweeter as the years pass.

In fact, Larry and I celebrated our 46th anniversary, January 20-21, 2002. We renewed our vows in church with our pastor, in the presence of family, friends, and church family.

We are more like bride and groom now than when we first took our vows. I am healed from the sexual abuse, deception, and rejection. We also forgave each other of all the emotional turmoil we brought into the marriage. We came into this marriage at the wrong time, but since then we have invited Christ to be head of our lives, our marriage, and to make us one-flesh. After that everything started falling into its proper place in our relationship.

Our lives started as a large puzzle with several pieces missing. Jesus, the Holy Spirit, the Word of God, and both of us being committed to God were the missing pieces in our marriage. In spite of misconception and disagreements, with God's help we are working out our problems. I am free of past hurts, and secret sins, because they are under the blood of Jesus Christ. Since my wall came down, there is a big change in our relationship. We have been praying for God to make us one and bring us into agreement. He has answered our prayer. Often as a thought comes to my mind Larry speaks the same thing. Many times when I speak, he says that's exactly what he is thinking.

The reason for sharing this testimony is for the sake of ministry. If this story will help other hurting women enter into the joy of the Lord, then it is worth all of the hurt, and hardship that I experienced. Always remember that the joy of the Lord is our strength; He is our help in the time of need. I was like many others, really in need of joy. I cried out to God, and He rescued me. We don't have to stay in captivity because Jesus died so we can be free. He will rescue all that want out of their situation. If you have unforgiveness, anger, rejection, low self-esteem or depression, Jesus will set you free also, and give you joy. Through believing in Jesus Christ, and accepting him as Savior and Lord, one can be made whole. I have learned that when I made a decision to forgive others and myself, it set me free. Through this freedom I have learned to walk in God's joy and peace, regardless of what others do or say to me. When we are grounded in God's word, we will be like trees whose roots grow deep. When a strong wind or storm blows it might lean, but seldom is it pull up by the root.

Likewise, storms of life might come against us, but it can't pull us away from God's peace and joy. This joy and peace can be like the sea on a stormy day. The waves can be high and rough on the top, but deep down in the sea the waters are calm. We can have tranquility in spite of chaos around us when our relationships are right with God. We allow others to have too much control over us when our joy and peace depend on their action. God desires us to be controlled by the Holy Spirit, instead of others action. I accepted the facts that my joy depends on my disposition. Jesus validated me and assured me that I am a child of God. When we seek God for the mind of Christ it will help our mental outlook. Many women may have had experiences that caused hurt those hurts can go away if they turn to God for help.

All real peace and joy comes from the God of hope. We can have both if we believe in His Word. But after believing, we must put the Word into action daily in our lives. God is pleased when we walk in forgiveness and treat others like we want them to treat us. God will take care of those who harm us when we do our part, and leave his part to him. Our job is to lift up Jesus in every situation; when the world sees our Godly reaction when we experience ungodly treatment, it will cause them to want what we have. According to the Word of God, we are to pray for those that mistreat us. When we do what God says, then we can trust Him to fix the problem. God is much better at taking care of evildoers than us; most times we make matters worse.

Trouble will not last always; we must look up and live our lives to the fullness in God, set our affection on things above that we might have His joy.

"Weeping may endure for a night, but joy cometh in the morning," (Psalms 30:5, KJV).

The word of God promises that joy will come in the morning. Therefore, joy will come when we have the right state of mind regarding the situation in relationship to God's promises. If we lack joy in our life we can leap for joy. If we believe God's word when it states leap for joy it will come. Shouting for joy is stated many times in the Old Testament. We must shout or leap for joy, instead of waiting for joy to come then shout. An example of shouting for joy was when the people of Jerusalem gather on one accord for the laying of the foundation of the temple. "When the foundation of this house was laid before their eyes, wept with a loud voice; and many shouted aloud for joy," (Ezra 3:12, KJV):

If we keep our attitude right, obey the word of God, be filled with His Holy Spirit, take our mind off what people think of us, and leap for joy, it will come. There is strength in God's joy. "For the joy of the Lord is my strength," (Nehemiah 8:10b, KJV). If the trouble of the world hurts, and depression, low self-esteem, worry or despair is getting to you, just begin to shout for joy, because His joy is our strength.

We don't have to settle for a little joy; we can have the fullness of joy if that's our desire. It is truly up to us what we want from God. I know it is His will for us to have joy because it is a fruit of the Holy Spirit. When we are filled with God's Holy Spirit, joy comes with it. The devil tries to steal our joy. When he does, shout for joy, and it will manifest. Once we are filled with the Holy Spirit, walk in divine love, and live in complete obedience to God's word, then walking in joy is a choice. I am striving for complete obedience. When one gets to that level of obedience, it will come with much persecution. In spite of that, God still provides a way for us to have joy. God gives us careful instruction concerning when we are persecuted for righteous sake.

Please read these instructions carefully.
"Blessed are ye, when men shall hate you, and when they shall separate you from their company, and shall reproach you, and cast out your name as evil, for the Son of man's sake. Rejoice ye in that day, and leap for joy: for, behold, your reward is great in heaven, (Luke 6:22-23a, KJV)."

Joy is a choice. We have choices when we are hurt, rejected, or forsaken for Christ sake: We can feel sorry for ourselves and have our own personal pity party. We can invite other to come to the pity party by complaining. We can get angry and strike out to defend ourselves.

We can remember that Jesus and other great men and women of God, suffered before us. He was rejected for us, beaten, shed blood, and died on the cross that we might have everlasting life. Follow his instruction; leap for joy.

Leaping for joy involves more than mere jumping up and down. Joy comes when our disposition lines up with the Word of God. Leaping and praising God instead of getting angry when we are persecuted for Christ's sake is how I keep my joy. Everything in my life is not perfect, but when I leap for joy I am filled with unspeakable joy and God's glory. I am learning that each experience, whether positive or negative, can be a learning experience.

If we learn the lesson from each experience it will mean growth, and we can move on with our lives in a positive way with peace and joy. If we don't learn the lesson from the experience, we will keep moving around in the same circle, taking the same test over again. The longer it takes us to learn the lesson, the greater the suffering. When I inquire of

God concerning what lesson is in an experience for me, He lets me know.

Many times I have learned that it is something in me that God wants to reveal. Once He reveals what needs fixing and I repent, then I have learned the lesson. Many times God allows people to come into our lives because we need such person to rub us the wrong way to get the rough edges smooth in us. It is necessary to keep seeking God, reading His Word and abide in it, or the old person will come alive in me. I pause every once in a while to thank God for bringing me through many disappointments. In spite of the past suffering, with God's help and mercy, I came through the ranks.

What have I learned on my journey From Jilt to Joy? God only allows things to happen to me that He will work for my good. I learned to pull down the walls that I built trying to protect myself from being hurt. When we build walls to protect ourselves by being too independent, we shut others out and hinder the Holy Spirit from protecting us. When we don't yield to God for his protection, this allows Satan to place his demons to stand guard, and he doesn't have our best interests in mind. I learned never to hold on to hurts. Turn problems over to God as soon as possible. He can handle them better than I.

Be quick to forgive. Unforgiveness puts an overload on my system. God loves the abusers and cares about their souls as well as mine.

I also learned to thank God in all circumstances because He cares for me and enables me to enter into His joy.

My prayer is that God will bless each reader to pursue His joy, by shouting, leaping, walking in forgiveness, living a fruitful, and victorious life. Pursue Joy. Jesus loves you!

Epilogue

By seeking God, trusting in Him, interviewing people from various walks of life, doing research, and my life experiences have qualified me to write this book, From Jilt to Joy.

I hope my descendants pass on guidance, faith, and endurance just as my ancestors passed on to me. Make your decision what you want to pass to the next generation that they may be blessed.

"Blessed is the man that endure temptation: for when he is tried, he shall receive the crown of life, which the Lord hath promised to them that love Him", (James 1:12, KJV).

Endure! As long as we live there will be some problems that will need to be solved, because we are human. As I approach the end of my journey, I want to leave with you a lamp (the Word of God), to guide your steps. Jesus is the Light of the world and no problem is too hard for Him. Keep the faith, endure temptation, and pass the Light to others.

I hope through this book I have made clear the message that God has provided for deliverance for hurting souls.

End Notes

1. Diane E. Papalia and Sally Wendkos Olds, *A Child's World*. The McGraw Hill Company, 1966, p. 479.

2. Charles Stanley, *Expriencing Forgiveness*. Thomas Nelson Publishers, 1982, p. 68.

3. James Strong, *The New Strong's Exhaustive Concordance of the Bible*. Copyright © Thomas Nelson Publishers, 1955, p. 329. Used by permission of Thomas Nelson, Inc.

Correction: "*Strong Concordance*" mentioned on page 106 should read "*New Strong's Exhaustive Concordance.*"